OUR COUNTRY'S GOOD

by Timberlake Wertenbaker

based on The Playmaker, a novel by Thomas Keneally

The Royal Court Writers Series
Published by Methuen
in association with The Royal Court Theatre

THE ROYAL COURT WRITERS SERIES

First published in Great Britain as a Methuen Paperback original in 1988 by
Methuen Drama, Michelin House, 81 Fulham Road, London SW3 6RB
in association with The Royal Court Theatre, Sloane Square, London SW1

This edition reprinted with revisions in 1989
Copyright © 1988, 1989 by Timberlake Wertenbaker based on the novel
The Playmaker by Thomas Keneally © 1987 The Serpentine Publishing Company Pty,
published by Hodder and Stoughton and Sceptre.

British Library Cataloguing in Publication Data

    Wertenbaker, Timberlake
      Our country's good: based on the novel
      The playmaker by Thomas Keneally.———
      (The Royal Court writers series).
      I. Title   II. Keneally, Thomas. Playmaker.
      III. Royal Court Theatre   IV. Series
      812'.64

      ISBN 0-413-19770-7

Set and printed by Expression Printers Ltd, London N7 9DP

COMING NEXT

IN THE MAIN HOUSE   730 1745

Sunday September 10th

The Downshire Players of London
Associate Orchestra at the Royal Court Theatre present

A CONCERT OF MUSIC BY SCARLATTI AND HANDEL

Harpsicord: David Wray Soprano: Rosa Mannion

From October 6
The Royal Court Theatre and Diana Bliss present

APPLES

The Musical by Ian Dury Directed by Simon Curtis

APPLES is Ian Dury's first musical. It is a vision of contemporary life seen through the eyes of Byline Brown, a tabloid journalist. Brown is on the trail of a major scandal in high places which involves drop outs, low lives and a sinister minister.

IN THE THEATRE UPSTAIRS 730 2554

August 24 — September 16
The Royal Court Theatre in association with Issac Davidov present

BLOOD

by Harwant S. Bains Directed by Lindsay Posner

BLOOD begins amidst the horrific carnage of the Indian Partition of 1947. It follows the journey of two young sikhs from their small, rural community in the Punjab to the Britain of the 1960's. There they find lucrative work, but also an increasing sense of dislocation.

September 27 — October 21
The Royal Court Theatre presents the Warehouse Theatre, Croydon, production of

THE ASTRONOMER'S GARDEN

by Kevin Hood Directed by Ted Craig

The Royal Observatory, in 1717, is the setting for this exploration of dangerous passions and obsessive desires.
Flamsteed, the Astronomer Royal, surrounded by his frustrated wife, an unscrupulous maid and an ambitious assistant, jealously attempts to guard his discoveries with the arrival in Greenwich of his arch enemy and eventual successor, Edward Halley.

November 15 December 9
The Warehouse Theatre, Croydon, and the Royal Court Theatre present

SLEEPING NIGHTIE

by Victoria Hardie

The play explores the themes of motherhood, child abuse and male violence and their effect on present and future generations. A lover is discovered through the eye of a camera; dark secrets are revealed in the bright light of a video show . . .

The Royal Court Theatre
and Diana Bliss present

OUR COUNTRY'S GOOD

BY TIMBERLAKE WERTENBAKER

based on Thomas Keneally's novel THE PLAYMAKER

CAPTAIN ARTHUR PHILLIP, RN, Governor-in-Chief of New South Wales ....Ron Cook
MAJOR ROBBIE ROSS, RM .... Mark Lambert
CAPTAIN DAVID COLLINS, RM, Advocate General .... Nigel Cooke
CAPTAIN WATKIN TENCH, RM .... Jude Akuwudike
CAPTAIN JEMMY CAMPBELL, RM..Clive Russell
REVEREND JOHNSON..Amanda Redman
LIEUTENANT GEORGE JOHNSTON, RM....................................Suzanne Packer
LIEUTENANT WILL DAWES, RM... Kathryn Hunter
2ND LIEUTENANT RALPH CLARK, RM......................................Julian Wadham
2ND LIEUTENANT WILLIAM FADDY, RM .... Mossie Smith
MIDSHIPMAN HARRY BREWER, RN, Provost Marshal ....Clive Russell
AN ABORIGINAL AUSTRALIAN.. Jude Akuwudike
JOHN ARSCOTT...Clive Russell
BLACK CAESAR .... Jude Akuwudike
KETCH FREEMAN .... Mark Lambert
ROBERT SIDEWAY.. Nigel Cooke
JOHN WISEHAMMER ....Ron Cook
MARY BRENHAM..Amanda Redman
DABBY BRYANT.. Mossie Smith
LIZ MORDEN .... Kathryn Hunter
DUCKLING SMITH ....Suzanne Packer
MEG LONG ....Amanda Redman

Directed by .... Max Stafford-Clark
Designed by... Peter Hartwell
Lighting Design.. Jenny Cane
Sound by... Bryan Bowen
Costume Supervisor .... Jennifer Cook
Fight Arranger... Terry King
Assistant Director.. Philip Howard
Company Manager.. Neil O'Malley
Stage Manager .... Jude Wheway
Assistant Stage Manager .... Gary Crant
Poster.. Sightlines
Production photos .... John Haynes

The play takes place in Sydney, Australia in 1788/89
There will be one interval of 15 minutes

Thanks to the Women's Playhouse Trust who helped take
THE RECRUITING OFFICER and OUR COUNTRY'S GOOD to Australia.

Wardrobe care by PERSIL and BIO-TEX. Adhesive by COPYDEX and EVODE LTD. Ioniser
for the lighting control room by THE LONDON IONISER CENTRE (836 0211). Cordless drill
by MAKITA ELECTRIC (UK) LTD. Watches by THE TIMEX CORPORATION. Batteries by EVER
READY. Refrigerators by ELECTROLUX and PHILLIPS MAJOR APPLIANCES LTD. Microwaves
by TOSHIBA UK LTD. Kettles for rehearsals by MORPHY RICHARDS. Video for casting
purposes by HITACHI. Cold bottled beers at the bar supplied by YOUNG & CO. BREWERY,
WANDSWORTH. Coffee machines by CONA.

SCENE TITLES

THE FULL COMPANY ON CLARK ISLAND, SYDNEY, AUSTRALIA JUNE 1989

BIOGRAPHIES

JUDE AKUWUDIKE — For the Royal Court: *The Recruiting Officer* and *Our Country's Good*. Other theatre includes: *The Park* (Sheffield Crucible); *Moon on a Rainbow Shawl* (Almeida); *The Fatherland* (Riverside). Film: *A World Apart*.

JENNY CANE — Recent lighting designs include: *Journey's End* (Whitehall); *The School for Scandal* (Theatre Royal, Plymouth); *King's Rhapsody* and *Time and Time Again* (Churchill, Bromley); *The Fit Up* (Nuffield, Southampton); *Exclusive Yarns* (Comedy Theatre); *Iolanthe* and *The Yeoman of the Guard* (Cambridge Theatre); *Dangerous Obsession* (Fortune); *Falstaff* (Oxford Stage Company); *Fiddler on the Roof* (Plymouth); *The Birth of Merlin* (Theatr Clwyd).

RON COOK — For the Royal Court: *The Arbor, Cloud Nine, The Grass Widow, Greenland, The Recruiting Officer* and *Our Country's Good*. Other theatre includes: *Sons of Light, Television Times, The Winter's Tale, The Crucible, The Dillen* (RSC); *She Stoops to Conquer* (Lyric, Hammersmith); *Ecstasy* and *How I Got That Story* (Hampstead); *Cock-Ups* (Royal Exchange, Manchester); *Three Sisters* (Greenwich/Albery). TV includes: *The Merry Wives of Windsor, A Day to Remember, The Singing Detective, The Miser, Bergerac*. Films: *The Cook, The Thief, His Wife and Her Lover, Number One*.

NIGEL COOKE — For the Royal Court: *Serious Money*, (at Wyndhams). Other theatre includes: seasons at Bristol Old Vic, the Little Theatre, Bristol, Basingstoke, Bolton, Scarborough; *The Public* (Stratford East); *The Duchess of Malfi* (Roundhouse); for the RSC: *Twelfth Night, Julius Caesar, Volpone*. TV includes: *Galloping Galaxies* and *Death of a Son*. Film: *Try Me*.

PETER HARTWELL — For the Royal Court: *The Glad Hand, Wheelchair Willie, Not Quite Jerusalem, The Genius, A Colder Climate, The Arbor*, The Edward Bond Season, *Operation Bad Apple, The Grass Widow, The Recruiting Officer, Our Country's Good, Icecream*. At the Royal Court and Public Theater, New York: *Rat in the Skull, Top Girls, Aunt Dan and Lemon, Serious Money* (also on Broadway). At the Theatre Upstairs: *An Empty Desk, Marie and Bruce, Seduced*. For Joint Stock: *Epsom Downs, Cloud Nine, The Ragged Trousered Philanthropists, Borderline, Crimes of Vautrin*. Other theatre includes: *She Stoops to Conquer, The Beaux' Stratagem* (Lyric, Hammersmith); *Serjeant Musgrave's Dance* (National); *Delicatessen* (Half Moon Theatre). Also work for Hampstead Theatre Club, Foco Novo, Newcastle and Liverpool Playhouses and the Canadian Stage Company, Toronto.

KATHRYN HUNTER — Theatre includes: *Romeo and Juliet* and *Merchant of Venice* (Watermill); *The Square* and *Yes, Peut-etre* (Edinburgh Festival); *A Little Like Drowning* (Hampstead); *The Hypochondriac* (Lyric, Hammersmith)l *Electra* and *All's Well that Ends Well* (Leicester Haymarket); *Abel Barebone, Playing with Fire, Noah's Wife* (Traverse, Edinburgh); *Anything for a Quiet Life* and *The Visit* (Theatre de Complicite/Almeida).

MARK LAMBERT — For the Royal Court: *Ourselves Alone, Built on Sand, The Recruiting Officer* and *Our Country's Good*. Other theatre credits include: *Red, Black and Ignorant* and *Juno and the Paycock* (RSC); *Patrick Pearse Motel* (Abbey Theatre); *Observe the Sons of Ulster Marching Towards the Somme* (Abbey Theatre and Hampstead); *Comedians* (Young Vic); *Candy Kisses* (The Bush). TV includes: *Caught in a Free State, The Young Ones, An Affair in Mind, Time After Time*. Films: *Champions* and *Prayer for the Dying*.

SUZANNE PACKER — For the Royal Court: *A Hero's Welcome*. Other theatre includes: *Topsey Turvey, Younger Brother's Son, Meg and Mog* (Unicorn); *Carmen Jones* and *Lady Be Good* (Crucible, Sheffield); *Power of Darkness, Playboy of the West Indies, Dreams with Teeth, To Kill a Mockingbird* (Contact, Manchester); *Little Shop of Horrors* (Leeds Playhouse); *Porgy and Bess* (Glyndebourne); *Fat Pig* (Leicester Haymarket); *To Kill a Mockingbird* (Greenwich); *Holly and the Magical Oak* (Brighton); *A Blow to Bute Street* (Cardiff). TV includes: *Bowen*.

AMANDA REDMAN — Theatre includes: *The Seagull, As You Like It, Destiny, A Month in the Country, Love for Love* (Bristol Old Vic); *The Rocky Horror Show, Windy City* (West End); *Crimes of the Heart* (Bush); *The Duenna* and *Swan Esther* (Young Vic); *Private Lives* (Oxford); *State of Affairs* (Lyric, Hammersmith); *Love for Love* (National); *The Last Waltz* (Greenwich). TV includes: *La Ronde, Pericles, Oxbridge Blues, To Have and to Hold, The Rivals, Bergerac, The Importance of Being Earnest, Streets Apart, The Lorelei*. Films include: *Richard's Things, Give My Regards to Broad Street, For Queen and Country*.

CLIVE RUSSELL — For the Royal Court: *Keeping Body and Sould Together*. Other theatre includes: Nine years in TIE/Community Theatre; *Kiss and Kill, Scum, Teendreams* (Monstrous Regiment); *Accidental Death of an Anarchist* (Wyndhams); *Hamlet, Waiting for Godot, A Streetcar Named Desire, Enemy of the People* (Lancaster); *Dracula, Scrap, The Erpingham Camp, Macbeth, Alfie* (Liverpool); *No Paseran, Macbeth, A View from the Bridge* (Young Vic); *King Lear* (Old Vic); for the RSC: *Philistines, The Dillen, Troilus and Cressida, Mephisto, Heresies, Principae Scriptorae, Fashion, New Inn, A Question of Geography, The Bite of the Night*. TV includes: *Boys from the Blackstuff, Anarchist, Tumbledown* and *The Gift*.

MOSSIE SMITH — For the Royal Court: *Shirley, Road, The Recruiting Officer, Our Country's Good*. Other theatre includes: *The Crucible* (Young Vic). TV includes: *Triangles, Number 10, Reith, Rat in the Skull, Putting on the Ritz, Road* and *A Very Peculiar Practice*.

MAX STAFFORD-CLARK — Like George Farquhar, Max Stafford-Clark is a graduate of Trinity College, Dublin. He was Artistic Director of the Traverse Theatre, Edinburgh, from 1968-1970. In 1972 he founded the Joint Stock Theatre Group and in 1979 he became Artistic Director of the Royal Court.

JULIAN WADHAM — For the Royal Court: *Serious Money, Falkland Sound, Young Writers' Festival*. Other theatre includes: *Mountain Language, The Changeling* (National Theatre); *When We Are Married, Another Country* (West End); also seasons at Chichester, Ipswich, Leatherhead, Leeds. TV includes: *Blind Justice, Baal, Country, Bright Eyes, The Guest, Bergerac, The Gentle Touch*. Films: *Mountbatten — the Last Viceroy* and *Maurice*.

LETTERS TO GEORGE

By Max Stafford-Clark

In August, Nick Hern Books will publish Max Stafford-Clark's first book, *Letters to George*. It takes the form of a correspondence with the author of *The Recruiting Officer*. In this book, Max traces the process of research and rehearsal on both *The Recruiting Officer* and Timberlake Wertenbaker's *Our Country's Good*.

Monday 9th July, 1988
End of Fifth Week

Dear George,

During the course of last week all the cast have been to Her Majesty's Prison, Wormwood Scrubs, to see a performance by the prisoners of Howard Barker's *Love of a Good Man*. I went tonight for the final performance. The prisoner/actors had been supplemented by two professional actresses, and by one professional actor. Howard's play had been deemed unsuitable for consumption by fellow prisoners, so the audience was stuffed with theatrical potentates invited by the ILEA. Half the audience seemed to be casting directors. There was Mary Selway, hello Patsy Pollock. I learned afterwards that the professional actors were rather overawed by this unanticipated event. From being a rather peculiar fringe gig, this job had become a major showcase opportunity. I'd never been in a prison before. Fielding once said nobody who had been to an English public school would ever feel out of place in a prison. How right; through the second airlock and it was immediately familiar territory. It was like playing an away match at one of the rather rugged schools, like Sedbergh, where they all wear shorts the whole time. It smelt of disinfectant and bottled male misery.

The production was clear and simple, with a minimum of props and lights. The prisoners weren't exactly hard to spot. Two of them were very striking indeed; tall, thin and incredibly pale, they looked like skinny plants forced to shoot up to find the light. They performed with varying degrees of skill but with intense focus and commitment. The play didn't have the frequent references to dripping genitalia that characterise most of Howard's work, but it wasn't lacking in robust sexual expression either: "I'd like to kiss your white arse," murmured the gangling, pale intense prisoner as he clasped his hands on the neatly suited buttocks of the extremely attractive actress (Eve White). As his mouth hovered close to hers the charge was tangible. It was difficult to watch. The actors' pride in their work and their pleasure in the achievement was thrilling. Above all, the evening was a heady confirmation of how sexy plays are. Keneally spotted that and, of course, he's absolutely right. In an atmosphere of repression and constraint where sex is forbidden, the play becomes a conduit for sexuality. In *The Recruiting Officer* most of the characters are horny most of the time. Given that it remained one of the few expressions of independence for the prisoners too, the rehearsals in Australia must have been crackling with sexual energy.

After the performance there was an opportunity to meet the actors for about ten minutes before they were led back to D-Wing. They were eager to talk. There was no shyness or hanging back. Joe, clearly the star of the evening, had been accused of killing his best friend when on an LSD trip. I asked him if he wanted to be an actor when he got out. He said he did. I was about to introduce him to Patsy Pollock when I thought to ask when he got out. "Ten to fifteen years", he said. There didn't seem such a hurry for him to meet Patsy after all. The part of the effete Prince Edward had been played by a chunky, black cockney who had been a body-builder before he came in. He had killed a bloke who had been harassing his sister. Onstage, he seemed charming, witty and rather camp. Offstage, I realised this had been character work of a high order. He was still charming, but definitely not the kind of bloke whose drink you would want to spill in the pub. The men said things like: "Rehearsing is the only time you're not in prison". They had clearly been obsessed with rehearsing, and wholehearted approval from professionals gave them huge pleasure. They could rehearse for an hour and a half two or three times a week. But rehearsals were often cancelled as screws declined to volunteer for the extra duty, or there simply wasn't enough prison staff.

I asked when they were going to do another play. Joe didn't know; he said he could be transferred at any time. He expected to go to Wakefield and there were no drama facilities there. It seemed heartbreaking to awaken this talent and then deny him the possibility of using it. Up close they had a real prison pallor; that's how convicts must have looked when they landed at Sydney Cove after eight months in the hold. They were very emotional. It was, after all, their final performance, and they had been rehearsing since just after Christmas. Joe made a very moving speech thanking the director, Alan McCormack. As they were led away we applauded again; their commitment seemed courageous in this context.

Afterwards we met the professional actors and the director in the prison officers' bar just outside the gates. This was a shock too. It was Saturday night and a country-and-western band was playing. The lead singer was dressed as a scantily clad cowgirl. Somehow the sound of this jollity drifting back to the men, now locked in their cells, was disturbing. Alan McCormack said: "It's the screws that make the prison terrible; they don't think the prisoners should get applause. They're there to be punished. If the prisoners enjoy themselves that's not on". Exactly the same arguments have been used in our officers' mess scene in *Our Country's Good*. He said the sense of achieving something provided tremendous therapy for the cons: "It's total liberation for them". One problem of directing them was getting them to play anger: " . . . the last time they lost their temper they probably killed somebody".

An hour or so later I left to go home. As I walked to the car I could hear the prisoners shouting from cell to cell through the warm night. I stopped and listened. Theatre is a savage god, that year by year takes more from you than it ever gives back, but it can be potent and thrilling. And it rewards you when you least expect it.

An extract from *Letters to George* — the account of a rehearsal.
Copyright © 1989 by Max Stafford-Clark.
Published by Nick Hern Books, 87 Vauxhall Walk, London SE11.

TIMBERLAKE WERTENBAKER   A break in *Our Country's Good* rehearsals.

Following the first production of *Our Country's Good*, I received
this letter from Joe White who had played Hacker in *Love of a Good Man*
at Wormwood Scrubs. It is reprinted here with his kind permission. T W

N55463 J. White
D Wing
H.M.P. Blundeston
Lowestoft
Suffolk NP32 5BG

April 1989

Dear Timberlake,

It seems an age since the production of *Love of a Good Man* at 'The Scrubs'. Within a couple of months the 'inside' cast was split up and moved to various far-flung parts of the country.

Firstly, a belated congratulations on your award for *Our Country's Good*. I did manage to have a read of the script; Eve White — one of the actresses — brought a copy in for us to read. Of course, I'd much rather have been able to see a performance, but, there you go. Reading through the play, there were moments of ghostly familiarity, uncanny likenesses.

Secondly, the compliments you gave to our play in the various reviews of *Our Country's Good* did not pass unnoticed. Not to mention the 'plug' you gave us all on actually receiving your award. It is difficult for me to explain the sense of achievement and feelings of pride it gave not only myself and the rest of the cast, but also to our families and friends. It spoke volumes. Thank you.

Mac, who played the Prince of Wales in *Love of* . . . was moved to a prison in the Isle of Sheppey, where he is making moves to start a drama group. Here at Blundeston, I was lucky enough to meet up with a fellow 'lifer' that I'd previously acted with in another 'Scrubs' production — Steven Berkoff's *East*. Lee subsequently wrote a play *Timecycles* about prison life, based around some of Steve's material. We set to work getting it put on here. I had a bash at directing, and I'm happy to say the first (of many, hopefully) Blundeston plays was performed last month to the rest of the guys in here. It was quite an experience for all concerned. You wouldn't believe the amount of energy and patience needed to get it together. Maybe you would — a universal aspect of theatre?

Basically the spirit lives on. Prison is about failure normally, and how we are reminded of it each day of every year. Drama, and self-expression in general, is a refuge and one of the only real weapons against the hopelessness of these places. I believe you gained the insight to recognise this, it is evident in your writing.

Theatre is, of course, an essential part of all society, and I'm glad to say that it is alive and kicking within these walls. Long may it do so. Again many, many thanks, and I look forward to reading more of your work.

Yours sincerely,

[signature: Joe White]

JOE WHITE

Laurence Olivier 1907-1989

THE OLIVIER APPEAL

The Royal Court Theatre was very proud of Lord Olivier's patronage of our Appeal. It will continue in his name as a memorial to his life and talent.

The Appeal was launched in June 1988 — The Royal Court's 100th anniversary year. The target is £800,000 to repair and refurbish the theatre and to enable the English Stage Company to maintain and continue its worldwide reputation as Britain's 'National Theatre of new writing'.

The Royal Court would like to thank the following for their generous contributions to the Appeal:

Jeffrey Archer
Edgar Astaire
Associated British Foods
Andrew Bainbridge
The Clifford Barclay Trust
Phyllis Blackburn
The Elaine and Neville Blond Charitable Trust
Paul Brooke
Isador Caplan
Peter Carter
Geoffrey Chater
Graham Cowley
David Crosner
The Douglas Heath Eves Trust
Douglas Fairbanks
The Economist
The Esmee Fairbairn Trust
Matthew Evans
Evans and Reiss
Robert Fleming Bank
D J Freeman & Company
Brian Friel
Michael Frayn
Gala (100th Anniversary)
The Godinton Trust
Caroline Goodall
Lord Goodman
Roger Graef
Christopher Hampton
Hatter (IMO) Foundation

The Hedley Trust
Claude Hug
Mr. & Mrs. Trevor John
The John Lewis Partnership
The Kobler Trust
The London and Edinburgh Trust
The Mercers
National Westminster Bank
Anna Louise Neuberg Trust
Olivier Banquet
A.J.G. Patenall
Pirelli Ltd.
A.J.R. Purssell
Mr. & Mrs. J.A. Pye's Charitable Settlement
St. Quentin Ltd.
The Rayne Foundation
The Lord Sainsbury Trust
Save & Prosper Group
Paul Schofield
Andrew Sinclair
D. R. Slack
W.H. Smith & Son
The Spencer-Wills Trust
Max Stafford-Clark
'Stormy Monday' Charity Premiere
Mary Trevelyan
Andrew Wadsworth
Womens Playhouse Trust
Sandra Yarwood

THE ROYAL COURT THEATRE SOCIETY

For many years now Members of the Royal Court Theatre Society have received special notice of new productions, but why not become a **Friend, Associate** or a **Patron of the Royal Court**, thereby involving yourself directly in maintaining the high standard and unique quality of Royal Court productions — while enjoying complimentary tickets to the shows themselves? Subscriptions run for one year; to become a Member costs £10, a Friend £50 (joint)/£35 (single), an Associate £350, a Patron £1,000.

PATRONS
Jeffrey Archer, Diana Bliss, Caryl Churchill, Issac Davidov, Alfred Davis, Mr. & Mrs. Nicholas Egon, Mrs. Henny Gestetner, Lady Eileen Joseph, Henry Kaye, Tracey Ullman, Julian Wadham.

ASSOCIATES
Peter Boizot, David Capelli, Michael Codron, Jeremy Conway, Stephen Fry, Elizabeth Garvie, The Earl of Gowrie, David Hart, London Arts Discovery Tours, Patricia Marmont, Barbara Minto, Greville Poke, Michael Serlin, Sir Dermot de Trafford, Nick Hern Books, Richard Wilson.

FRIENDS
Paul Adams, Roger Allam & Susan Todd, Robin Anderson, Jane Annakin, John Arthur, Mrs. M. Bagust, Martine Baker, Linda Bassett, Paul Bater, Josephine Beddoe, Laura Birkett, Anthony Blond, Bob Boas, Irving H. Brecker, Katie Bradford, Jim Broadbent, Alan Brodie, Ralph Brown, A.J.H. Buckley, Stuart Burge, Nell Goodhue Cady, Laurence Cann, Susan Card, Guy Chapman, Steve Childs, Ruby Cohn, Angela Coles, Sandra Cook, Lynn & Bernhard Cottrell, Lou Coulson, Peter Cregeen, Harriet Cruickshank, B. R. Cuzner, Mrs. Der Pao Graham, Anne Devlin, Mrs. V.A. Dimant, Julia Dos Santos, R.H. & B.H. Dowler, Adrian Charles Dunbar, Susan Dunnett, Pamela Edwardes, George A. Elliott III, Jan Evans, Trevor Eve, Kenneth Ewing, Leonard Fenton, Mr. & Mrs. Thomas Fenton, Kate Feast, M.H. Flash, Robert Fox, Gilly Fraser, David Gant, Kerry Gardner, Anne Garwood, Sarah Garner, Alfred Molina & Jill Gascoine, Jonathan Gems, Frank & Woji Gero, Beth Goddard, Lord Goodman, Joan Grahame, Roger Graef, Rod Hall, Sharon Hamper, Shahab Hanif, A.M. Harrison, Vivien Heilbron, Jan Harvey, Peter Headill, Sarah Hellings, Jocelyn Herbert, Ashley & Pauline Hill, David Horovitch, Dusty Hughes, Vi Hughes, Diana Hull, Susan Imhof, Trevor Ingman, Kenny Ireland, Jonathan Isaacs, Alison E. Jackson, Richard Jackson, Dick Jarrett, B. E. Jenkins, Hugh Jenkins, Dominic Jephcott, Paul Jesson, Donald Jones, Dr. & Mrs. David Josefowitz, Elizabeth Karr Tashman, Sharon Kean, Alice Kennelly, Jean Knox, Sir Kerry & Lady St. Johnston, Mrs. O. Lahr, Dr. R.J. Lande, Iain Lanyon, Hugh Laurie, Alison Leathart, Peter Ledeboer, Sheila Lemon, Peter L. Levy, Robert S. Linton, Mr & Mrs M. M. Littman, Roger & Moira Lubbock, John & Erica Macdonald, Suzie Mackenzie, Marina Mahler, Paul Mari, Rosy Nasreen & Dr. Conal Liam Mannion, Marina Martin, Patricia Marx, Anna Massey, S. A. Mason, Paul Matthews, Elaine Maycock, Philip L. McDonald, Ian McMillan, James Midgley, Louise Miller, Anthony Minghella, L.A.G. Morris, T. Murnaghan, Alex Nash, Linda Newns, Sally Newton, John Nicholls, Michael Nyman, Nick Marston, Richard O'Brien, Eileen & John O'Keefe, Stephen Oliver, Gary Olsen, Mark Padmore, Norma Papp, Alan David & Jane Penrose, Ronald Pickup, Pauline Pinder, Harold Pinter, Nigel Planer, Laura Plumb, Peter Polkinghorne, Trevor Preston, R. Puttick, Margaret Ramsay, Jane Rayne, B.J. & Rosmarie Reynolds, E.W. Richards, Alan Rickman, David Robb, Martin & Jennifer Roddy, Christie Ryan, George Scheider, Rosemary Squire, A.J. Sayers, Leah Schmidt, Martin & Glynis Scurr, Jennifer Sebag-Montefiore, Mrs. L.M. Sieff, Paul Sinclair Brooke, Andrew Sinclair and Sonia Melchett, Ms. A.M. Jamieson & Mr. A.P. Smith, Peter A. Smith, Jane Snowden, Max Stafford-Clark, Louise Stein, Jenny Stein, Jeff Steltzer, Lindsay Stevens, Pearl Stewart, Richard Stokes, Richard Stone, Rob Sutherland, Dudley Sutton, Audrey & Gordon Taylor, Steve Tedbury, Nigel Terry, Mary Trevelyan, Amanda and R. L. W. Triggs, Elizabeth Troop, Mrs. Anne Underwood, Kiomars Vejdani, Maureen Vincent, Karen and Wes Wadman, Andrew Wadsworth, Harriet Walter, Julie Walters, Tim Watson, Nicholas Wright, Charles & Victoria Wright.

FOR THE ROYAL COURT

DIRECTION

Artistic Director	MAX STAFFORD-CLARK
Deputy Director	SIMON CURTIS
Casting Director	LISA MAKIN
Literary Manager	KATE HARWOOD
Assistant Director	PHILIP HOWARD
Artistic Assistant	MELANIE KENYON
Arts Council Writer in Residence	CLARE McINTYRE

PRODUCTION

Production Manager	BO BARTON
Chief Electrician	COLIN ROXBOROUGH
Deputy Chief Electrician	JAMES ARMSTRONG
Electrician	DENIS O'HARE*
Sound Designer	BRYAN BOWEN
Board Operators	STEVE HEPWORTH*
Master Carpenter	CHRIS BAGUST
Deputy Master Carpenter	ALAN JOYCE
Wardrobe Supervisor	JENNIFER COOK
Deputy Wardrobe Supervisor	CATHIE SKILBECK

ADMINISTRATION

General Manager	GRAHAM COWLEY
Assistant to General Manager	LUCY WOOLLATT
Finance Administrator	STEPHEN MORRIS
Finance Assistant	RACHEL HARRISON
Press (730 2652)	TAMSIN THOMAS
Marketing & Publicity Manager	GUY CHAPMAN
Development Director	TOM PETZAL
Development Assistant	JACQUELINE VIEIRA
House Manager	WILLIAM DAY
Deputy House Manager	ALISON SMITH
Bookshop	ANGELA TOULMIN*
Box Office Manager	GILL RUSSELL
Box Office Assistants	GERALD BROOKING, RITA SHARMA
Stage Door/Telephonists	ANGELA TOULMIN, JAN NOYCE*
Evening Stage Door	TYRONE LUCAS*
Maintenance	JOHN LORRIGIO
Cleaners	EILEEN CHAPMAN*, IVY JONES*
Firemen	PAUL KLEINMANN*, DAVID WYATT*

YOUNG PEOPLE'S THEATRE

Director	ELYSE DODGSON
Administrator	DOMINIC TICKELL
Youth and Community Worker	EUTON DALY

*Part-time staff

COUNCIL: Chairman: MATTHEW EVANS, CHRIS BAGUST, BO BARTON, STUART BURGE, ANTHONY C. BURTON, CARYL CHURCHILL, BRIAN COX, HARRIET CRUICKSHANK, SIMON CURTIS, ALLAN DAVIS, DAVID LLOYD DAVIS, ROBERT FOX, MRS. HENNY GESTETNER OBE, DEREK GRANGER, DAVID HARE, JOCELYN HERBERT, DAVID KLEEMAN, HANIF KUREISHI, SONIA MELCHETT, JAMES MIDGLEY, JOAN PLOWRIGHT CBE, GREVILLE POKE, RICHARD PULFORD, JANE RAYNE, JIM TANNER, SIR HUGH WILLATT.

This Theatre is associated with the Regional Theatre Young Directors Scheme.

Twenty per cent of the children in a certain elementary school were reported to their teachers as showing unusual potential for intellectual growth. The names of these twenty per cent of the children were drawn by means of a table of random numbers, which is to say that the names were drawn out of a hat. Eight months later these unusual or 'magic' children showed significantly greater gains in IQ than did the remaining children who had not been singled out for the teachers' attention. The change in the teachers' expectations regarding the intellectual performance of these allegedly 'special' children had led to an actual change in the intellectual performance of these randomly selected children . . . who were also described as more interesting, as showing greater intellectual curiosity and as happier.

R. Rosenthal & L. Jacobsen *Pygmalion in the Classroom*

OUR
COUNTRY'S
GOOD

ACT ONE

Scene One

The Voyage Out

The hold of a convict ship bound for Australia, 1787. The convicts huddle together in the semi-darkness. On deck, the convict ROBERT SIDEWAY is being flogged. SECOND LIEUTENANT RALPH CLARK counts the lashes in a barely audible, slow and monotonous voice.

RALPH CLARK: Forty-four, forty-five, forty-six, forty-seven, forty-eight, forty-nine, fifty.

SIDEWAY is untied and dumped with the rest of the convicts. He collapses. No one moves. A short silence.

JOHN WISEHAMMER: At night? The sea cracks against the ship. Fear whispers, screams, falls silent, hushed. Spewed from our country, forgotten, bound to the dark edge of the earth, at night what is there to do but seek English cunt, warm, moist, soft, oh the comfort, the comfort of the lick, the thrust into the nooks, the crannies of the crooks of England. Alone, frightened, nameless in this stinking hole of hell, take me, take me inside you, whoever you are. Take me, my comfort and we'll remember England together.

Scene Two

A lone Aboriginal Australian describes the arrival of the First Convict Fleet in Botany Bay on January 20, 1788.

THE ABORIGINE: A giant canoe drifts onto the sea, clouds billowing from upright oars. This is a dream which has lost its way. Best to leave it alone.

Scene Three

Punishment

Sydney Cove: GOVERNOR ARTHUR PHILLIP, JUDGE DAVID COLLINS, CAPTAIN WATKIN TENCH, MIDSHIPMAN HARRY BREWER. *The men are shooting birds.*

PHILLIP: Was it necessary to cross fifteen thousand miles of ocean to erect another Tyburn?

TENCH: I should think it would make the convicts feel at home.

COLLINS: This land is under English law. The court found them guilty and sentenced them accordingly. There: a bald-eyed corella.

PHILLIP: But hanging?

COLLINS: Only the three who were found guilty of stealing from the colony's stores. And that, over there on the Eucalyptus, is a flock of 'cacatua galerita' – the sulphur-crested cockatoo. You have been made Governor-in-Chief of a paradise of birds, Arthur.

PHILLIP: And I hope not of a human hell, Davey. Don't shoot yet, Watkin, let's observe them. Could we not be more humane?

TENCH: Justice and humaneness have never gone hand in hand. The law is not a sentimental comedy.

PHILLIP: I am not suggesting they go without punishment. It is the spectacle of hanging I object to. The convicts will feel nothing has changed and will go back to their old ways.

TENCH: The convicts never left their old ways, Governor, nor do they intend to.

PHILLIP: Three months is not long enough to decide that. You're speaking too loud, Watkin.

COLLINS: I commend your endeavour to oppose the baneful influence of vice with the harmonising acts of civilisation, Governor, but I suspect your edifice will collapse without the mortar of fear.

PHILLIP: Have these men lost all fear of being flogged?

COLLINS: John Arscott has already been sentenced to 150 lashes for assault.

TENCH: The shoulder blades are exposed at about 100 lashes and I would say that somewhere between 250 and 500 lashes you are probably condemning a man to death anyway.

COLLINS: With the disadvantage that the death is slow, unobserved and cannot serve as a sharp example.

PHILLIP: Harry?

HARRY: The convicts laugh at hangings, Sir. They watch them all the time.

TENCH: It's their favourite form of entertainment, I should say.

PHILLIP: Perhaps because they've never been offered anything else.

TENCH: Perhaps we should build an opera house for the convicts.

PHILLIP: We learned to love such things because they were offered to us when we were children or young men. Surely no one is born naturally cultured? I'll have the gun now.

COLLINS: We don't even have any books here, apart from the odd play and a few Bibles. And most of the convicts can't read, so let us return to the matter in hand, which is the punishment of the convicts, not their education.

PHILLIP: Who are the condemned men, Harry?

HARRY: Thomas Barrett, age 17. Transported seven years for stealing one ewe sheep.

PHILLIP: Seventeen!

TENCH: It does seem to prove that the criminal tendency is innate.

PHILLIP: It proves nothing.

HARRY: James Freeman, age 25, Irish, transported 14 years for assault on a sailor at Shadwell Dock.

COLLINS: I'm surprised he wasn't hanged in England.

HARRY: Handy Baker, marine and the thieves' ringleader.

COLLINS: He pleaded that it was wrong to put the convicts and the marines on the same rations and that he could not work on so little food. He almost swayed us.

TENCH: I do think that was an unfortunate decision, Governor. My men are in a ferment of discontent.

COLLINS: Our Governor-in-Chief would say it is justice, Tench, and so it is. It is also justice to hang these men.

TENCH: The sooner the better, I believe. There is much excitement in the colony about the hangings. It's their theatre, Governor, you cannot change that.

PHILLIP: I would prefer them to see real plays: fine language, sentiment.

TENCH: No doubt Garrick would relish the prospect of eight months at sea for the pleasure of entertaining a group of criminals and the odd savage.

PHILLIP: I never liked Garrick, I always preferred Macklin.

COLLINS: I'm a Kemble man myself. We will need a hangman.

PHILLIP: Harry, you will have to organise the hangings and eventually find someone who agrees to fill that hideous office.

PHILLIP *shoots.*

COLLINS: Shot.

TENCH: Shot.

HARRY: Shot, sir.

COLLINS: It is my belief the hangings should take place tomorrow. The quick execution of justice for the good of the colony, Governor.

PHILLIP: The good of the colony? Oh, look! We've frightened a kankaroo.

HARRY: There is also Dorothy Handland, 82, who stole a biscuit from Robert Sideway.

PHILLIP: Surely we don't have to hang an 82-year-old woman?

COLLINS: That will be unnecessary. She hanged herself this morning.

Scene Four

The Loneliness of Men

RALPH CLARK's tent. It is late at night. RALPH stands, composing and speaking his diary

RALPH: Dreamt, my beloved Alicia, that I was walking with you and that you was in your riding-habit – oh my dear woman when shall I be able to hear from you –
    All the officers dined with the Governor – I never heard of any one single person having so great a power vested in him as Captain Phillip has by his commission as Governor-in-Chief of New South Wales – dined on a cold collation but the Mutton which had been killed yesterday morning was full of maggots – nothing will keep 24 hours in this dismal country I find –
    Went out shooting after breakfast – I only shot one cockatoo – they are the most beautiful birds –
    Major Ross ordered one of the Corporals to flog with a rope Elizabeth Morden for being impertinent to Captain Campbell – the Corporal did not play with her but laid it home which I was very glad to see – she has long been fishing for it –
    On Sunday as usual, kissed your dear beloved image a thousand times – was very much frightened by the lightning as it broke very near my tent – several of the convicts have run away.

He goes to his table and writes in his journal.

If I'm not made 1st Lieutenant soon . . .

HARRY BREWER *has come in.*

RALPH: Harry –

HARRY: I saw the light in your tent –

RALPH: I was writing my journal.

Silence.

Is there any trouble?

HARRY: No. (*Pause.*)
    I just came.
    Talk, you know. If I wrote a journal about my life it would fill volumes. Volumes. My travels with the Captain – His Excellency now, no less, Governor-in-Chief, power to raise armies, build cities – I still call him plain Captain Phillip. He likes it from me. The war in

America and before that, Ralph, my life in London. That would fill a volume on its own. Not what you would call a good life.

Pause.

Sometimes I look at the convicts and I think, one of those could be you, Harry Brewer, if you hadn't joined the navy when you did. The officers may look down on me now, but what if they found out that I used to be an embezzler?

RALPH: Harry, you should keep these things to yourself.

HARRY: You're right, Ralph.

Pause.

I think the Captain suspects, but he's a good man and he looks for different things in a man –

RALPH: Like what?

HARRY: Hard to say. He likes to see something unusual.
    Ralph, I saw Handy Baker last night.

RALPH: You hanged him a month ago, Harry.

HARRY: He had a rope – Ralph, he's come back.

RALPH: It was a dream. Sometimes I think my dreams are real – But they're not.

HARRY: We used to hear you on the ship, calling for your Betsey Alicia.

RALPH: Don't speak her name on this iniquitous shore!

HARRY: Duckling's gone silent on me again. I know it's because of Handy Baker. I saw him as well as I see you. Duckling wants me, he said, even if you've hanged me. At least your poker's danced its last shindy, I said. At least it's young and straight, he said, she likes that. I went for him but he was gone. But he's going to come back, I know it. I didn't want to hang him, Ralph, I didn't.

RALPH: He did steal that food from the stores.

Pause.

I voted with the rest of the court those men should be hanged, I didn't know His Excellency would be against it.

HARRY: Duckling says she never feels anything. How do I know she didn't feel something when she was with him? She thinks I hanged him to get rid of him, but I didn't, Ralph.

Pause.

Do you know I saved her life? She was sentenced to be hanged at Newgate for stealing two silver candlesticks but I got her name put on the transport lists. But when I remind her of that she says she wouldn't have cared. Eighteen years old, and she didn't care if she was turned off.

Pause.

These women are sold before they're ten. The Captain says we should treat them with kindness.

RALPH: How can you treat such women with kindness? Why does he think that?

HARRY: Not all the officers find them disgusting, Ralph – haven't you ever been tempted?

RALPH: Never! (*Pause.*) His Excellency never seems to notice me.

Pause.

He finds time for Davey Collins, Lieutenant Dawes.

HARRY: That's because Captain Collins is going to write about the customs of the Indians here – and Lieutenant Dawes is recording the stars.

RALPH: I could write about the Indians.

HARRY: He did suggest to Captain Tench that we do something to educate the convicts, put on a play or something, but Captain Tench just laughed. He doesn't like Captain Tench.

RALPH: A play? Who would act in a play?

HARRY: The convicts of course. He is thinking of talking to Lieutenant Johnston, but I think Lieutenant Johnston wants to study the plants.

RALPH: I read 'The Tragedy of Lady Jane Grey' on the ship. It is such a moving and uplifting play. But how could a whore play Lady Jane?

HARRY: Some of those women are good

women, Ralph, I believe my Duckling is good. It's not her fault – if only she would look at me, once, react. Who wants to fuck a corpse!

Silence.

I'm sorry. I didn't mean to shock you, Ralph, I have shocked you, haven't I? I'll go.

RALPH: Is His Excellency serious about putting on a play?

HARRY: When the Captain decides something, Ralph.

RALPH: If I went to him – no, it would be better if you did, Harry, you could tell His Excellency how much I like the theatre.

HARRY: I didn't know that Ralph, I'll tell him.

RALPH: Duckling could be in it, if you wanted.

HARRY: I wouldn't want her to be looked at by all the men.

RALPH: If His Excellency doesn't like Lady Jane we could find something else.

Pause.

A comedy perhaps . . .

HARRY: I'll speak to him, Ralph. I like you.

Pause.

It's good to talk . . .

Pause.

You don't think I killed him then?

RALPH: Who?

HARRY: Handy Baker.

RALPH: No, Harry. You did not kill Handy Baker.

HARRY: Thank you, Ralph.

RALPH: Harry, you won't forget to talk to His Excellency about the play?

Scene Five

An Audition

RALPH CLARK, MEG LONG.

MEG LONG *is very old and very smelly. She hovers over* RALPH.

MEG: We heard you was looking for some women, Lieutenant. Here I am.

RALPH: I've asked to see some women to play certain parts in a play.

MEG: I can play, Lieutenant, I can play with any part you like. There ain't nothing puts Meg off. That's how I got my name: Shitty Meg.

CLARK: The play has four particular parts for young women.

MEG: You don't want a young woman for your peculiar, Lieutenant, they don't know nothing. Shut your eyes and I'll play you as tight as a virgin.

RALPH: You don't understand, Long. Here's the play. It's called 'The Recruiting Officer'.

MEG: Oh, I can do that too.

RALPH: What?

MEG: Recruiting. Anybody you like. (*She whispers.*) You want women: you ask Meg. Who do you want?

RALPH: I want to try some out.

MEG: Good idea, Lieutenant, good idea. Ha! Ha! Ha!

RALPH: Now if you don't mind –

MEG *doesn't move.*

RALPH: Long!

MEG (*frightened, but still holding her ground*): We thought you was a madge cull. Ha! Ha!

RALPH: What?

MEG: You know, a fluter, a mollie. (*Impatiently.*) A prissy cove, a girl! You having no she-lag on the ship. Nor here, neither. On the ship maybe you was seasick. But all these months here. And now we hear how you want a lot of women, all at once. Well, I'm glad to hear that, Lieutenant, I am. You let me know when you want Meg, old shitty Meg. Ha! Ha!

She goes off quickly and ROBERT SIDEWAY *comes straight on.*

SIDEWAY: Ah, Mr Clark.

He does a flourish.

I am calling you Mr Clark as one calls Mr Garrick Mr Garrick, we have not had the pleasure of meeting before.

RALPH: I've seen you on the ship.

SIDEWAY: Different circumstances, Mr Clark, best forgotten. I was once a gentleman. My fortune has turned. The wheel . . . You are doing a play, I hear, ah, Drury Lane, Mr Garrick, the lovely Peg Woffington. (*Conspiratorially.*) He was so cruel to her. She was so pale –

CLARK: You say you were a gentleman, Sideway?

SIDEWAY: Top of my profession, Mr Clark, pickpocket, born and bred in Bermondsey. Do you know London, Sir, don't you miss it? In these my darkest hours, I remember my happy days in that great city. London Bridge at dawn – hand on cold iron for good luck. Down Cheapside with the market traders – never refuse a mince pie. Into St Paul's Churchyard – I do love a good Church – and begin work in Bond Street. There, I've spotted her, rich, plump, not of the best class, stands in front of the shop, plucking up courage, I pluck her. Time for coffee until five o'clock and the pinnacle, the glory of the day: Drury Lane. The coaches, the actors scuttling, the gentlemen watching, the ladies tittering, the perfumes, the clothes, the handkerchiefs.

He hands RALPH *the handkerchief he has just stolen from him.*

Here, Mr Clark, you see the skill. Ah, Mr Clark, I beg you, I entreat you, to let me perform on your stage, to let me feel once again the thrill of a play about to begin. Ah, I see ladies approaching: our future Woffingtons, Siddons.

DABBY BRYANT *comes on, with a shrinking* MARY BRENHAM *in tow.* SIDEWAY *bows.*

Ladies.
I shall await your word of command, Mr Clark, I shall be in the wings.

SIDEWAY *scuttles off.*

DABBY: You asked to see Mary Brenham, Lieutenant. Here she is.

RALPH: Yes – the Governor has asked me to put on a play. (*To* MARY.) You know what a play is?

DABBY: I've seen lots of plays, Lieutenant, so has Mary.

RALPH: Have you Brenham?

MARY (*inaudibly*): Yes.

RALPH: Can you remember which plays you've seen?

MARY (*inaudibly*): No.

DABBY: I can't remember what they were called, but I always knew when they were going to end badly. I knew right from the beginning. How does this one end, Lieutenant?

RALPH: It ends happily. It's called 'The Recruiting Officer'.

DABBY: Mary wants to be in your play, Lieutenant, and so do I.

RALPH: Do you think you have a talent for acting, Brenham?

DABBY: Of course she does, and so do I. I want to play Mary's friend.

RALPH: Do you know 'The Recruiting Officer', Bryant?

DABBY: No, but in all those plays, there's always a friend. That's because a girl has to talk to someone and she talks to her friend. So I'll be Mary's friend.

RALPH: Silvia – that's the part I want to try Brenham for – doesn't have a friend. She has a cousin. But they don't like each other.

DABBY: Oh. Mary doesn't always like me.

RALPH: The Reverend Johnson told me you can read and write, Brenham?

DABBY: She went to school until she was ten. She used to read to us on the ship. We loved it. It put us to sleep.

RALPH: Shall we try reading some of the play?

RALPH *hands her the book.* MARY *reads silently, moving her lips.*

RALPH: I meant read it aloud. As you did on the ship. I'll help you, I'll read Justice Balance. That's your father.

DABBY: Doesn't she have a sweetheart?

RALPH: Yes, but this scene is with her father.

DABBY: What's the name of her lover?

RALPH: Captain Plume.

DABBY: A Captain! Mary!

RALPH: Start here, Brenham.

MARY *begins to read.*

MARY: 'Whilst there is life there is hope, sir'.

DABBY: Oh, I like that, Lieutenant. This is a good play, I can tell.

RALPH: Shht. She hasn't finished. Start again, Brenham, that's good.

MARY: 'Whilst there is life there is hope, sir; perhaps my brother may recover.'

RALPH: That's excellent Brenham, very fluent. You could read a little louder. Now I'll read.

'We have but little reason to expect it. Poor Owen! But the decree is just; I was pleased with the death of my father, because he left me an estate, and now I'm punished with the loss of an heir to inherit mine.'

Pause. He laughs a little.

This is a comedy. They don't really mean it. It's to make people laugh. 'The death of your brother makes you sole heiress to my estate, which you know is about twelve hundred pounds a year.'

DABBY: Twelve hundred pounds! It must be a comedy.

MARY: 'My desire of being punctual in my obedience requires that you would be plain in your commands, sir.'

DABBY: Well said, Mary, well said.

RALPH: I think that's enough. You read very well, Brenham. Would you also be able to copy the play? We have only two copies.

DABBY: Course she will. Where do I come in, Lieutenant? The cousin.

RALPH: Can you read, Bryant?

DABBY: Not those marks in the books, Lieutenant, but I can read other things. I read dreams very well, Lieutenant. Very well.

RALPH: I don't think you're right for Melinda. I'm thinking of someone else. And if you can't read . . .

DABBY: Mary will read me the lines, Lieutenant.

RALPH: There's Rose . . .

DABBY: Rose. I like the name. I'll be Rose. Who is she?

RALPH: She's a country girl . . .

DABBY: I grew up in Devon, Lieutenant. I'm perfect for Rose. What does she do?

RALPH: She – well, it's complicated. She falls in love with Silvia.

MARY begins to giggle but tries to hold it back.

RALPH: But it's because she thinks Silvia's a man. And she – they – she sleeps with her. Rose. With Silvia. Euh. Silvia too. With Rose. But nothing happens.

DABBY: It doesn't? Nothing?

DABBY bursts out laughing.

RALPH: Because Silvia is pretending to be a man, but of course she can't –

DABBY: Play the flute? Ha! She's not the only one around here. I'll do Rose.

RALPH: I would like to hear you.

DABBY: I don't know my lines yet, Lieutenant. When I know my lines, you can hear me do them. Come on, Mary –

RALPH: I didn't say you could – I'm not certain you're the right – Bryant, I'm not certain I want you in the play.

DABBY: Yes you do, Lieutenant. Mary will read me the lines and I, Lieutenant, will read you your dreams.

There's a guffaw. It's LIZ MORDEN.

RALPH: Ah. Here's your cousin.

There is a silence. MARY shrinks away. DABBY and LIZ stare at each other, each holding her ground, each ready to pounce.

RALPH: Melinda. Silvia's cousin.

DABBY: You can't have her in the play, Lieutenant.

RALPH: Why not?

DABBY: You don't have to be able to read the future to know that Liz Morden is going to be hanged.

LIZ looks briefly at DABBY, as if to strike, then changes her mind.

LIZ: I understand you want me in your play, Lieutenant. Is that it?

She grabs the books from RALPH and strides off.

I'll look at it and let you know.

Scene Six

The Authorities Discuss the Merits of the Theatre

GOVERNOR ARTHUR PHILLIP, MAJOR ROBBIE ROSS, JUDGE DAVID COLLINS, CAPTAIN WATKIN TENCH, CAPTAIN JEMMY CAMPBELL, REVEREND JOHNSON, LIEUTENANT GEORGE JOHNSTON, LIEUTENANT WILL DAWES, LIEUTENANT RALPH CLARK, LIEUTENANT WILLIAM FADDY.

It is late at night, the men have been drinking, tempers are high. They interrupt each other, overlap, make jokes under and over the conversation but all engage in it with the passion for discourse and thought of eighteenth-century men.

ROSS: A play! A f –

REVD. JOHNSON: Mmhm.

MAJOR ROSS: A frippery frittering play!

CAMPBELL: Aheeh, aeh, here?

RALPH (*timidly*): To celebrate the King's Birthday, on June the 4th.

ROSS: If a frigating ship doesn't appear soon, we'll all be struck with stricturing starvation – and you – you – a play!

COLLINS: Not putting on the play, won't bring us a supply ship, Robbie.

ROSS: And you say you want those contumelious convicts to act in this play.

The convicts!

CAMPBELL: Eh, kev, weh, discipline's bad. Very bad.

RALPH: The play has several parts for women. We have no other women here.

COLLINS: Your wife excepted, Reverend.

REVD. JOHNSON: My wife abhors anything of that nature. After all, actresses are not famed for their morals.

COLLINS: Neither are our women convicts.

REVD. JOHNSON: How can they be when some of our officers set them up as mistresses.

He looks pointedly at LIEUTENANT GEORGE JOHNSTON.

ROSS: Filthy, thieving, lying whores and now we have to watch them flout their flitty wares on the stage!

PHILLIP: No one will be forced to watch the play.

DAWES: I believe there's a partial lunar eclipse that night. I will have to watch that. The sky of this southern hemisphere is full of wonders. Have you looked at the constellations?

Short pause.

ROSS: Constellations! Plays! This is a convict colony, the prisoners are here to be punished and we're here to make sure they get punished. Constellations! Jemmy?

He turns to JEMMY CAMPBELL *for support.*

CAMPBELL: Tss, weh, marines, marines: war, phoo, discipline. Eh? Service – His Majesty.

PHILLIP: We are indeed here to supervise the convicts who are already being punished by their long exile. Surely they can also be reformed?

TENCH: We are talking about criminals, often hardened criminals. They have a habit of vice and crime. Habits are difficult to break. And it can be more than habit, an innate tendency. Many criminals seem to have been born that way. It is in their nature.

PHILLIP: Rousseau would say that we have

made them that way, Watkin: 'Man is born free, and everywhere he is in chains'.

REVD. JOHNSON: But Rousseau was a Frenchman.

ROSS: A Frenchman! What can you expect? We're going to listen to a foraging Frenchman now –

COLLINS: He was Swiss actually.

CAMPBELL: Eeh, eyeh, good soldiers, the Swiss.

PHILLIP: Surely you believe man can be redeemed, Reverend?

REVD. JOHNSON: By the grace of God and a belief in the true church, yes. But Christ never proposed putting on plays to his disciples. However, he didn't forbid it either. It must depend on the play.

JOHNSTON: He did propose treating sinners, especially women who have sinned, with compassion. Most of the convict women have committed small crimes, a tiny theft –

COLLINS: We know about your compassion, not to say passion, for the women convicts, George.

TENCH: A crime is a crime. You commit a crime or you don't. If you commit a crime, you are a criminal. Surely that is logical? It's like the savages here. A savage is a savage because he behaves in a savage manner. To expect anything else is foolish. They can't even build a proper canoe.

PHILLIP: They can be educated.

COLLINS: Actually, they seem happy enough as they are. They do not want to build canoes or houses, nor do they suffer from greed and ambition.

FADDY (*looking at* RALPH): Unlike some.

TENCH: Which can't be said of our convicts. But really, I don't see what this has to do with a play. It is at most a passable diversion, an entertainment to wile away the hours of the idle.

CAMPBELL: Ttts, weh, he, the convicts, bone idle.

DAWES: We're wiling away precious hours now. Put the play on, don't put it on, it won't change the shape of the universe.

RALPH: But it could change the nature of our little society.

FADDY: Second Lieutenant Clark change society!

PHILLIP: William!

TENCH: My dear Ralph, a bunch of convicts making fools of themselves, mouthing words written no doubt by some London Ass, will hardly change our society.

RALPH: George Farquhar was not an ass! And he was from Ireland.

ROSS: An Irishman! I have to sit there and listen to an Irishman!

CAMPBELL: Tss, tt. Irish. Wilde. Wilde.

REVD. JOHNSON: The play doesn't propagate Catholic doctrine, does it, Ralph?

RALPH: He was also an officer.

FADDY: Crawling for promotion.

RALPH: Of the grenadiers.

ROSS: Never liked the Grenadiers myself.

CAMPBELL: Ouah, pheuee, grenades, pho. Throw and run. Eh. Backs.

RALPH: The play is called 'The Recruiting Officer'.

COLLINS: I saw it in London I believe. Yes. Very funny if I remember. Sergeant Kite. The devious ways he used to serve his Captain . . .

FADDY: Your part, Ralph.

COLLINS: William, if you can't contribute anything useful to the discussion, keep quiet.

Silence.

REVD. JOHNSON: What is the plot, Ralph?

RALPH: It's about this recruiting officer and his friend, and they are in love with these two young ladies from Shrewsbury and after some difficulties, they marry them.

REVD. JOHNSON: It sanctions Holy Matrimony then?

RALPH: Yes, yes, it does.

REVD. JOHNSON: That wouldn't do the

convicts any harm. I'm having such trouble getting them to marry instead of this sordid cohabitation they're so used to.

ROSS: Marriage, plays, why not a ball for the convicts!

CAMPBELL: Euuh. Boxing.

PHILLIP: Some of these men will have finished their sentence in a few years. They will become members of society again, and help create a new society in this colony. Should we not encourage them now to think in a free and responsible manner?

TENCH: I don't see how a comedy about two lovers will do that, Arthur.

PHILLIP: The theatre is an expression of civilisation. We belong to a great country which has spawned great playwrights: Shakespeare, Marlowe, Jonson, and even in our own time, Sheridan. The convicts will be speaking a refined, literate language and expressing sentiments of a delicacy they are not used to. It will remind them that there is more to life than crime, punishment. And we, this colony of a few hundred will be watching this together, for a few hours we will no longer be despised prisoners and hated gaolers. We will laugh, we may be moved, we may even think a little. Can you suggest something else that will provide such an evening, Watkin?

DAWES: Mapping the stars gives me more enjoyment, personally.

TENCH: I'm not sure it's a good idea having the convicts laugh at officers, Arthur.

CAMPBELL: No. Pheeoh, insubordination, heh, ehh, no discipline.

ROSS: You want this vice-ridden vermin to enjoy themselves?

COLLINS: They would only laugh at Sergeant Kite.

RALPH: Captain Plume is a most attractive, noble fellow.

REVD. JOHNSON: He's not loose, is he Ralph? I hear many of these plays are about rakes and encourage loose morals in women. They do get married? Before, that is, before. And for the right reasons.

RALPH: They marry for love and to secure wealth.

REVD. JOHNSON: That's all right.

TENCH: I would simply say that if you want to build a civilisation there are more important things than a play. If you want to teach the convicts something, teach them to farm, to build houses, teach them a sense of respect for property, teach them thrift so they don't eat a week's rations in one night, but above all, teach them how to work, not how to sit around laughing at a comedy.

PHILLIP: The Greeks believed that it was a citizen's duty to watch a play. It was a kind of work in that it required attention, judgement, patience, all the social virtues.

TENCH: And the Greeks were conquered by the more practical Romans, Arthur.

COLLINS: Indeed, the Romans built their bridges, but they also spent many centuries wishing they were Greeks. And they, after all, were conquered by the barbarians, or by their own corrupt and small spirits.

TENCH: Are you saying Rome would not have fallen if the theatre had been better?

RALPH (*very loud*): Why not? (*Everyone looks at him and he continues, fast and nervously.*) In my own small way, in just a few hours, I have seen something change. I asked some of the convict women to read me some lines, these women who behave often no better than animals. And it seemed to me, as one or two – I'm not saying all of them, not at all – but one or two, saying those well-balanced lines of Mr Farquhar, they seemed to acquire a dignity, they seemed – they seemed to lose some of their corruption. There was one, Mary Brenham, she read so well, perhaps this play will keep her from selling herself to the first marine who offers her bread –

FADDY (*under his breath*): She'll sell herself to him, instead.

ROSS: So that's the way the wind blows –

CAMPBELL: Hooh. A tempest. Hooh.

RALPH (*over them*): I speak about her, but in a small way this could affect all the convicts and even ourselves, we could forget our worries about the supplies, the hangings and the floggings, and think of ourselves at the theatre, in London, with our wives and children, that is, we could, euh –

PHILLIP: Transcend –

RALPH: Transcend the darker, euh – transcend the –

JOHNSTON: Brutal –

RALPH: The brutality – remember our better nature and remember –

COLLINS: England.

RALPH: England.

A moment.

ROSS: Where did the wee Lieutenant learn to speak?

FADDY: He must have had one of his dreams.

TENCH (*over them*): You are making claims that cannot be substantiated, Ralph. It's two hours, possibly of amusement, possibly of boredom, and we will lose the labour of the convicts during the time they are learning the play. It's a waste, an unnecessary waste.

REVD. JOHNSON: I'm still concerned about the content.

TENCH: The content of a play is irrelevant.

ROSS: Even if it teaches insubordination, disobedience, revolution?

COLLINS: Since we have agreed it can do no harm, since it might, possibly, do some good, since the only person violently opposed to it is Major Ross for reasons he has not made quite clear, I suggest we allow Ralph to rehearse his play. Does anyone disagree?

ROSS: I – I –

COLLINS: We have taken your disagreement into account, Robbie.

CAMPBELL: Ah, eeh, I – I – (*He stops.*)

COLLINS: Thank you Captain Campbell. Dawes? Dawes, do come back to earth and honour us with your attention for a moment.

DAWES: What? No? Why not? As long as I don't have to watch it.

COLLINS: Johnston?

JOHNSTON: I'm for it.

COLLINS: Faddy?

FADDY: I'm against it.

COLLINS: Could you tell us why?

FADDY: I don't trust the director.

COLLINS: Tench?

TENCH: Waste of time.

COLLINS: The Reverend, our moral guide, has no objections.

REVD. JOHNSON: Of course I haven't read it.

TENCH: Davey, this is not an objective summing up, this is typical of your high-handed manner –

COLLINS: I don't think you're the one to accuse others of a high-handed manner, Watkin.

PHILLIP: Gentlemen, please.

COLLINS: Your Excellency, I believe, is for the play and I myself am convinced it will prove a most interesting experiment. So let us conclude with our good wishes to Ralph for a successful production.

ROSS: I will not accept this. You willy-wally wobbly words, Greeks, Romans, experiment, to get your own way. You don't take anything seriously, but I know this play – this play – order will become disorder. The theatre leads to threatening theory and you, Governor, you have His Majesty's commission to build castles, cities, raise armies, administer a military colony, not fandangle about with a lewdy play! I am going to write to the Admiralty about this. (*He goes.*)

PHILLIP: You are out of turn, Robbie.

CAMPBELL: Aah – eeh – a. Confusion. (*He goes.*)

DAWES: Why is Robbie so upset? So much fuss over a play.

JOHNSTON: Major Ross will never forgive you, Ralph.

COLLINS: I have summed up the feelings of the assembled company, Arthur, but the last word must be yours.

PHILLIP: The last word will be the play, gentlemen.

Scene Seven

Harry and Duckling Go Rowing.

HARRY BREWER, DUCKLING SMITH. HARRY *is rowing*. DUCKLING *is sulking*.

HARRY: It's almost beginning to look like a town. Look, Duckling, there's the Captain's house. I can see him in his garden.

HARRY *waves*. DUCKLING *doesn't turn around*.

Sydney. He could have found a better name. Mobsbury. Lagtown. Duckling Cove, eh?

HARRY *laughs*. DUCKLING *remains morose*.

The Captain said it had to be named after the Home Secretary. The courthouse looks impressive all in brick. There's Lieutenant Dawes' observatory. Why don't you look, Duckling?

DUCKLING *glances, then turns back*.

The trees look more friendly from here. Did you know the Eucalyptus tree can't be found anywhere else in the world? Captain Collins told me that. Isn't that interesting? Lieutenant Clark says the three orange trees on his island are doing well. It's the turnips he's worried about, he thinks they're being stolen and he's too busy with his play to go and have a look. Would you like to see the orange trees, Duckling?

DUCKLING *glowers*.

I thought you'd enjoy rowing to Ralph's island. I thought it would remind you of rowing on the Thames. Look how blue the water is, Duckling. Say something. Duckling!

DUCKLING: If I was rowing on the Thames, I'd be free.

HARRY: This isn't Newgate, Duckling.

DUCKLING: I wish it was.

HARRY: Duckling!

DUCKLING: At least the gaoler of Newgate left you alone and you could talk to people.

Pause.

HARRY: I let you talk to the women.

DUCKLING (*with contempt*): Esther Abrahams, Mary Brenham!

HARRY: They're good women.

DUCKLING: I don't have anything to say to those women, Harry. My friends are in the women's camp –

HARRY: It's not the women you're after in the women's camp, it's the marines who come looking for buttock. I know you, who do you have your eye on now, who, a soldier? Another marine, a corporal? Who, Duckling, who?

Pause.

You've found someone already, haven't you? Where do you go, on the beach? In my tent, like with Handy Baker, eh? Where, under the trees?

DUCKLING: You know I hate trees, don't be so filthy.

HARRY: Filthy, you're filthy, you filthy whore.

Pause.

I'm sorry, Duckling, please. Why can't you? – can't you just be with me?

Don't be angry. I'll do anything for you, you know that. What do you want, Duckling?

DUCKLING: I don't want to be watched all the time. I wake up in the middle of the night and you're watching me. What do you think I'm going to do in my sleep, Harry? Watching, watching, watching. JUST STOP WATCHING ME.

HARRY: You want to leave me. All right, go and live in the women's camp, sell yourself to a convict for a biscuit. Leave if you want to. You're filthy, filthy, opening your legs to the first marine –

DUCKLING: Why are you so angry with your Duckling, Harry? Don't you like it when I open my legs wide to you? Cross them over you – the way you like? What will you do when your little Duckling isn't there anymore to touch you with her soft fingertips, Harry, where you like it? First the left nipple and then the right. Your Duckling doesn't want to leave you, Harry.

HARRY: Duckling . . .

DUCKLING: I need freedom sometimes, Harry.

HARRY: You have to earn your freedom with good behaviour.

DUCKLING: Why didn't you let them hang me and take my corpse with you, Harry? You could have kept that in chains. I wish I was dead. At least when you're dead, you're free.

Silence.

HARRY: You know Lieutenant Clark's play?

DUCKLING *is silent.*

Do you want to be in it?

DUCKLING *laughs.*

Dabby Bryant is in it too and Liz Morden. Do you want to be in it?

You'd rehearse in the evenings with Lieutenant Clark.

DUCKLING: And he can watch over me instead of you.

HARRY: I'm trying to make you happy, Duckling, if you don't want to –

DUCKLING: I'll be in the play.

Pause.

How is Lieutenant Clark going to manage Liz Morden?

HARRY: The Captain wanted her to be in it.

DUCKLING: On the ship we used to see who could make Lieutenant Clark blush first. It didn't take long, haha.

HARRY: Duckling, you won't try anything with Lieutenant Clark, will you?

DUCKLING: With that mollie? No.

HARRY: You're talking to me again. Will you kiss your Harry?

They kiss.

I'll come and watch the rehearsals.

Scene Eight
The Women Learn Their Lines

DABBY BRYANT *is sitting on the ground muttering to herself with concentration. She could be counting.* MARY BRENHAM *comes on.*

MARY: Are you remembering your lines, Dabby?

DABBY: What lines? No. I was remembering Devon. I was on my way back to Bigbury Bay.

MARY: You promised Lieutenant Clark you'd learn your lines.

DABBY: I want to go back. I want to see a wall of stone. I want to hear the Atlantic breaking into the estuary. I can bring a boat into any harbour, in any weather. I can do it as well as the Governor.

MARY: Dabby, what about your lines?

DABBY: I'm not spending the rest of my life in this flat, brittle, burnt-out country. Oh, give me some English rain.

MARY: It rains here.

DABBY: It's not the same. I could recognise English rain anywhere. And Devon rain, Mary, Devon rain is the softest in England. As soft as your breasts, as soft as Lieutenant Clark's dimpled cheeks.

MARY: Dabby, don't!

DABBY: You're wasting time, girl, he's ripe for the plucking. You can always tell with men, they begin to walk sideways. And if you don't –

MARY: Don't start. I listened to you once before.

DABBY: What would you have done without that lanky sailor drooling over you?

MARY: I would have been less of a whore.

DABBY: Listen, my darling, you're only a virgin once. You can't go to a man and say, I'm a virgin except for this one lover I had.

After that, it doesn't matter how many men go through you.

MARY: I'll never wash the sin away.

DABBY: If God didn't want women to be whores he shouldn't have created men who pay for their bodies. While you were with your little sailor there were women in that stinking pit of a hold who had three men on them at once, men with the pox, men with the flux, men biting like dogs.

MARY: But if you don't agree to it, then you're not a whore, you're a martyr.

DABBY: You have to be a virgin to be a martyr, Mary, and you didn't come on that ship a virgin. 'A. H. I love thee to the heart', ha, way up there –

DABBY *begins to lift* MARY's *skirt to reveal a tattoo high up on the inner thigh.* MARY *leaps away.*

MARY: That was different. That was love.

DABBY: The second difficulty with being a martyr is that you have to be dead to qualify. Well, you didn't die, thanks to me, you had three pounds of beef a week instead of two, two extra ounces of cheese.

MARY: Which you were happy to eat!

DABBY: We women have to look after each other. Let's learn the lines.

MARY: You sold me that first day so you and your husband could eat!

DABBY: Do you want me to learn these lines or not?

MARY: How can I play Silvia? She's brave and strong. She couldn't have done what I've done.

DABBY: She didn't spend eight months and one week on a convict ship. Anyway, you can pretend you're her.

MARY: No. I have to be her.

DABBY: Why?

MARY: Because that's acting.

DABBY: No way I'm being Rose, she's an idiot.

MARY: It's not such a big part, it doesn't matter so much.

DABBY: You didn't tell me that before

MARY: I hadn't read it carefully. Come on, let's do the scene between Silvia and Rose. (*She reads.*) 'I have rested but indifferently, and I believe my bedfellow was as little pleased; poor Rose! Here she comes' –

DABBY: I could have done something for Rose. Ha! I should play Silvia.

MARY: 'Good morrow, my dear, how d'ye this morning?' Now you say: 'Just as I was last night, neither better nor worse for you.'

LIZ MORDEN *comes on.*

LIZ: You can't do the play without me. I'm in it! Where's the Lieutenant?

DABBY: She's teaching me some lines.

LIZ: Why aren't you teaching me the lines?

MARY: We're not doing your scenes.

LIZ: Well do them.

DABBY: You can read. You can read your own lines.

LIZ: I don't want to learn them on my own.

LIZ *thrusts* DABBY *away and sits by* MARY.

LIZ: I'm waiting.

DABBY: What are you waiting for, Liz Morden, a blind man to buy your wares?

MARY (*quickly*): We'll do the first scene between Melinda and Silvia, all right?

LIZ: Yea. The first scene.

MARY *gives* LIZ *the book.*

MARY: You start.

LIZ *looks at the book*

MARY: You start. 'Welcome to town, cousin Silvia' –

LIZ: 'Welcome to town, cousin Silvia' –

MARY: Go on – 'I envied you' –

LIZ: 'I envied you'. You read it first.

MARY: Why?

LIZ: I want to hear how you do it.

MARY: Why?

LIZ: 'Cause then I can do it different.

MARY: 'I envied you your retreat in the country; for Shrewsbury, methinks, and all your heads of shires –

LIZ: You're saying it too fast.

MARY: Well, you can say it slower.

LIZ: No. You do it slower, then I'll do it fast.

DABBY: Why don't you read it? You can't read!

LIZ: What?

She lunges at DABBY.

MARY: Liz. I'll teach you the lines.

DABBY: Are you her friend now, is that it? Mary the holy innocent and thieving bitch –

LIZ *and* DABBY *seize each other.* KETCH FREEMAN *appears.*

KETCH (*with nervous affability*): Good morning ladies. And why aren't you at work instead of at each other's throats.

LIZ *and* DABBY *turn on him.*

LIZ: I wouldn't talk of throats if I was you, Mr Hangman Ketch Freeman.

DABBY: Crap merchant.

LIZ: Crapping cull. Switcher.

MARY: Roper.

KETCH: I was only asking what you were doing, you know, friendly like.

LIZ: Stick to your ropes, my little galler, don't bother the actresses.

KETCH: Actresses?

Pause.

You're doing a play.

LIZ: Better than dancing the Paddington Frisk in your arms – noser!

KETCH: I'll nose on you, Liz, if you're not careful.

LIZ: I'd take a leap in the dark sooner than turn off my own kind. Now take your whirligigs out of our sight, we have lines to learn.

KETCH *slinks away as* LIZ *and* DABBY *spit him off.*

DABBY (*after him*): Don't hang too many people, Ketch, we need an audience!

MARY: 'Welcome to town, cousin Silvia.' It says you salute.

LIZ (*giving a military salute*): 'Welcome to town, cousin – Silvia.'

Scene Nine

Ralph Clark Tries to Kiss His Dear Wife's Picture

RALPH's *tent. Candlelight.* RALPH *paces.*

RALPH: Dreamt my beloved Betsey that I was with you and that I thought I was going to be arrested.

He looks at his watch.

I hope to God that there is nothing the matter with you my tender Alicia or that of our dear boy –

He looks at his watch.

My darling tender wife I am reading Proverbs waiting till midnight, the Sabbath, that I might kiss your picture as usual.

He takes his Bible and kneels. Looks at his watch.

The Patrols caught three seamen and a boy in the women's camp.

He reads:

'Let thy fountain be blessed: and rejoice with the wife of thy youth.'

Good God what a scene of whoredom is going on there in the women's camp.

He looks at his watch. Gets up. Paces.

Very hot this night.

Captain Shea killed today one of the Kankaroos – it is the most curious animal I ever saw.

He looks at his watch.

Almost midnight, my Betsey, the Lord's day –

He reads:

'And behold, there met him a woman with the attire of an harlot, and subtle of heart.

So she caught him, and kissed him with an impudent face.'

Felt ill with the toothache my dear wife my god what pain.

Reads:

'So she caught him and kissed him with an impudent face . . .'

I have perfumed my bed with myrrh, aloes, cinnamon –

Sarah McCormick was flogged today for calling the doctor a c – midnight –.

This being Sunday took your picture out of its prison and kissed it – God bless you my sweet woman.

He now proceeds to do so. That is, he goes down on his knees and brings the picture to himself.

KETCH FREEMAN *comes into the tent.* RALPH *jumps.*

KETCH: Forgive me, Sir, please forgive me, I didn't want to disturb your prayers. I say 50 Hail Mary's myself every night and 200 on the days when – I'll wait outside, Sir.

RALPH: What do you want?

KETCH: I'll wait quietly, Sir, don't mind me.

RALPH: Why aren't you in the camp at this hour?

KETCH: I should be, God forgive me, I should be, But I'm not. I'm here. I have to have a word with you, Sir.

RALPH: Get back to the camp immediately, I'll see you in the morning, Ketch.

KETCH: Don't call me that, Sir, I beg you, don't call me by that name, that's what I came to see you about, Sir.

RALPH: I was about to go to sleep.

KETCH: I understand, Sir, and your soul in peace, I won't take up your time, I'll be brief.

Pause.

RALPH: Well?

KETCH: Don't you want to finish your prayers? I can be very quiet. I used to watch my mother, may her poor soul rest in peace, I used to watch her say her prayers every night.

RALPH: Get on with it!

KETCH: When I say my prayers I have a terrible doubt. How can I be sure God is forgiving me? What if he will forgive me, but hasn't forgiven me yet? That's why I don't want to die, Sir. That's why I can't die. Not until I am sure. Are you sure?

RALPH: I'm not a convict: I don't sin.

KETCH: To be sure. Forgive me, Sir. But if we're in God's power, then surely he makes us sin. I was given a guardian angel when I was born, like all good Catholics, why didn't my guardian angel look after me better? But I think he must've stayed in Ireland. I think the devil tempted my mother to London and both our guardian angels stayed behind. Have you ever been to Ireland, Sir? It's a beautiful country. If I'd been an angel I wouldn't have left it either. And when we came within six fields of Westminister, the devils took over. But it's God's judgement I'm frightened of. And the women's. They're so hard. Why is that?

RALPH: Why have you come here?

KETCH: I'm coming to that, Sir.

RALPH: Hurry up, then.

KETCH: I'm speaking as fast as I can, Sir –

RALPH: Ketch –

KETCH: James, Sir, James, Daniel, Patrick, after my three uncles. Good men they were too, didn't go to London. If my mother hadn't brought us to London, may God give peace to her soul and breathe pity into the hearts of hard women – because the docks are in London and if I hadn't worked on the docks, on that day, May 23rd, 1785, do you remember it, Sir? Shadwell Dock. If only we hadn't left, then I wouldn't have been there, then nothing would have happened, I wouldn't have become a coal heaver on Shadwell Dock and been there on the 23rd of May when we refused to unload because they were paying us so badly Sir. I wasn't even near the sailor who got killed. He shouldn't have done the unloading, that was wrong of the sailors, but I didn't kill him, maybe one blow, not to look stupid, you know, just to show I was with the lads, even if I wasn't, but I didn't kill him. And they caught five at random Sir, and I was among the five, and they found the cudgel, but I just had that to look good, that's all, and when they said to me later you can hang or you can give the names what was I to do, what would you have done, Sir?

RALPH: I wouldn't have been in that situation, Freeman.

KETCH: To be sure, forgive me, Sir. I only told on the ones I saw, I didn't tell anything that wasn't true. Death is a horrible thing, that poor sailor.

RALPH: Freeman, I'm going to go to bed now–

KETCH: I understand, Sir, I understand. And when it happened again, here! And I had hopes of making a good life here. It's because I'm so friendly, see, so I go along, and then I'm the one who gets caught. That theft, I didn't do it, I was just there, keeping a look out, just to help some friends, you know. But when they say to you, hang or be hanged, what do you do? Someone has to do it. I try to do it well. God had mercy on the whore, the thief, the lame, surely he'll forgive the hang – it's the women – they're without mercy – not like you and me, Sir, men. What I wanted to say, Sir, is that I heard them talking about the play.

Pause.

Some players came into our village once. They were loved like the angels, Lieutenant, like the angels. And the way the women watched them – the light of a spring dawn in their eyes.

Lieutenant –

I want to be an actor.

Scene Ten

John Wisehammer and Mary Brenham Exchange Words

MARY *is copying 'The Recruiting Officer' in the afternoon light.* JOHN WISEHAMMER *is carrying bricks and piling them to one side. He begins to hover over her.*

MARY: 'I would rather counsel than command; I don't propose this with the authority of a parent, but as the advice of your friend' –

WISEHAMMER: Friend. That's a good word. Short, but full of promise.

MARY: 'That you would take the coach this moment and go into the country.'

WISEHAMMER: Country can mean opposite things. It renews you with trees and grass, you go rest in the country, or it crushes you with power: you die for your country, your country doesn't want you, you're thrown out of your country.

Pause.

I like words.

Pause.

My father cleared the houses of the dead to sell the old clothes to the poor houses by the Thames. He found a dictionary – Johnson's dictionary – it was as big as a Bible. It went from A to L. I started with the A's. Abecedarian: someone who teaches the alphabet or rudiments of literature. Abject: a man without hope.

MARY: What does indulgent mean?

WISEHAMMER: How is it used?

MARY (*reads*): 'You have been so careful, so indulgent to me' –

WISEHAMMER: It means ready to overlook faults.

Pause.

You have to be careful with words that begin with 'in'. It can turn everything upside down. Injustice. Most of that word is taken up with justice, but the 'in' twists it inside out and makes it the ugliest word in the English language.

MARY: Guilty is an uglier word.

WISEHAMMER: Innocent ought to be a beautiful word, but it isn't, it's full of sorrow. Anguish.

MARY *goes back to her copying.*

MARY: I don't have much time. We start this

in a few days.

WISEHAMMER *looks over her shoulder.*

MARY: I have the biggest part.

WISEHAMMER: You have a beautiful hand.

MARY: There is so much to copy. So many words.

WISEHAMMER: I can write.

MARY: Why don't you tell Lieutenant Clark? He's doing it.

WISEHAMMER: No . . . no . . . I'm –

MARY: Afraid?

WISEHAMMER: Diffident.

MARY: I'll tell him. Well, I won't. My friend Dabby will. She's –

WISEHAMMER: Bold.

Pause.

Shy is not a bad word, it's soft.

MARY: But shame is a hard one.

WISEHAMMER: Words with two L's are the worst. Lonely, loveless.

MARY: Love is a good word.

WISEHAMMER: That's because it only has one L. I like words with one L: Luck. Latitudinarian.

MARY *laughs.*

WISEHAMMER. Laughter.

Scene Eleven

The First Rehearsal

RALPH CLARK, ROBERT SIDEWAY, JOHN WISEHAMMER, MARY BRENHAM, LIZ MORDEN, DABBY BRYANT, DUCKLING SMITH, KETCH FREEMAN.

RALPH: Good afternoon, ladies and gentlemen –

DABBY: We're ladies now. Wait till I tell my husband I've become a lady.

MARY: Sshht.

RALPH: It is with pleasure that I welcome you –

SIDEWAY: Our pleasure, Mr Clark, our pleasure.

RALPH: We have many days of hard work ahead of us.

LIZ: Work! I'm not working. I thought we was acting.

RALPH: Now, let me introduce the company –

DABBY: We've all met before, Lieutenant, you could say we know each other, you could say we'd know each other in the dark.

SIDEWAY: It's a theatrical custom, the company is formally introduced to each other, Mrs Bryant.

DABBY: Mrs Bryant? Who's Mrs Bryant?

SIDEWAY: It's the theatrical form of address, madam. You may call me Mr Sideway.

RALPH: If I may proceed –

KETCH: Shhh! You're interrupting the director.

DABBY: So we are, Mr Hangman.

The women all hiss at KETCH.

RALPH: The ladies first: Mary Brenham who is to play Silvia. Liz Morden who is to play Melinda. Duckling Smith who is to play Lucy, Melinda's maid.

DUCKLING: I'm not playing Liz Morden's maid.

RALPH: Why not?

DUCKLING: I live with an officer. He wouldn't like it.

DABBY: Just because she lives chained up in that old toss pot's garden.

DUCKLING: Don't you dare talk of my Harry –

RALPH: You're not playing Morden's maid, Smith, you're playing Melinda's. And Dabby Bryant, who is to play Rose, a country girl.

DABBY: From Devon.

DUCKLING (*to* DABBY): Screw jaws!

DABBY (*to* DUCKLING): Salt bitch!

RALPH: That's the ladies. Now, Captain Plume will be played by Henry Kable.

He looks around.

Who seems to be late. That's odd. I saw him an hour ago and he said he was going to your hut to learn some lines, Wisehammer?

WISEHAMMER *is silent.*

Sergeant Kite is to be played by John Arscott, who did send a message to say he would be kept at work an extra hour.

DABBY: An hour! You won't see him in an hour!

LIZ (*under her breath*): You're not the only one with new wrinkles in your arse Dabby Bryant.

RALPH: Mr Worthy will be played by Mr Sideway.

SIDEWAY *takes a vast bow.*

SIDEWAY: I'm here.

RALPH: Justice Balance by James Freeman.

DUCKLING: No way I'm doing a play with a hangman. The words would stick in my throat.

More hisses and spitting. KETCH *shrinks.*

RALPH: You don't have any scenes with him, Smith. Now if I could finish the introductions. Captain Brazen is to be played by John Wisehammer.

The small parts are still to be cast. Now. We can't do the first scene until John Arscott appears.

DABBY: There won't be a first scene.

RALPH: Bryant, will you be quiet please! The second scene. Wisehammer, you could read Plume.

WISEHAMMER *comes forward eagerly.*

No, I'll read Plume myself. So, Act One, scene two, Captain Plume and Mr Worthy.

SIDEWAY: That's me. I'm at your command.

RALPH: The rest of you can watch and wait for your scenes. Perhaps we should begin by reading it.

SIDEWAY: No need, Mr Clark. I know it.

RALPH: Ah. I'm afraid I shall have to read Captain Plume.

SIDEWAY: I know that part too. Would you like me to do both?

RALPH: I think it's better if I do it. Shall we begin? Kite, that's John Arscott, has just left –

DABBY: Running.

RALPH: Bryant! I'll read the line before Worthy's entrance: 'None at present. 'Tis indeed the picture of Worthy, but the life's departed.' Sideway? Where's he gone?

SIDEWAY *has scuttled off. He shouts from the wings.*

SIDEWAY: I'm preparing my entrance, Mr Clark, I won't be a minute. Could you read the line again, slowly?

RALPH: ' 'Tis indeed the picture of Worthy, but the life's departed. What, arms-a-cross, Worthy!'

SIDEWAY *comes on, walking sideways, arms held up in a grandiose eighteenth-century theatrical pose. He suddenly stops.*

SIDEWAY: Ah, yes, I forgot. Arms-a-cross. I shall have to start again.

He goes off again and shouts.

Could you read the line again louder please.

RALPH: 'What, arms-a-cross, Worthy!'

SIDEWAY *rushes on.*

SIDEWAY: My wiper! Someone's buzzed my wiper! There's a wipe drawer in this crew, Mr Clark.

RALPH: What's the matter?

SIDEWAY: There's a pickpocket in the company.

DABBY: Talk of the pot calling the kettle black.

SIDEWAY *stalks around the company threateningly.*

SIDEWAY: My handkerchief. Who prigged my handkerchief?

RALPH: I'm sure it will turn up, Sideway, let's go on.

SIDEWAY: I can't do my entrance without my handerchief. (*Furious.*) I've been practising it all night. If I get my mittens on the rum diver I'll –

He lunges at LIZ who fights back viciously. They jump apart, each taking threatening poses and RALPH *intervenes with speed.*

RALPH: Let's assume Worthy has already entered, Sideway. Now, I say: 'What, arms-a-cross, Worthy! Methinks you should hold 'em open when a friend's so near. I must expel this melancholy spirit.'

SIDEWAY *has dropped to his knees and is sobbing in a pose of total sorrow.*

What are you doing down there, Sideway?

SIDEWAY: I'm being melancholy. I saw Mr Garrick being melancholy once. That is what he did. Hamlet it was.

He stretches his arms to the ground and begins to repeat.

'Oh that this too, too solid flesh would melt. Oh that this too too solid flesh would melt. Oh that this too too –'

RALPH: This is a comedy. It is perhaps a little lighter. Try simply to stand normally and look melancholy. I'll say the line again. (SIDEWAY *is still sobbing.*) The audience won't hear Captain Plume's lines if your sobs are so loud, Sideway.

SIDEWAY: I'm still establishing my melancholy.

RALPH: A comedy needs to move quite fast. In fact, I think we'll cut that line and the two verses that follow and go straight to Worthy greeting Plume.

WISEHAMMER: I like the word melancholy.

SIDEWAY: A greeting. Yes. A greeting looks like this.

He extends his arms high and wide.

'Plume!' Now I'll change to say the next words. 'My dear Captain', that's affection isn't it? If I put my hands on my heart, like this. Now, 'Welcome'. I'm not quite sure how to do 'Welcome'.

RALPH: I think if you just say the line.

SIDEWAY: Quite. Now.

He feels RALPH.

RALPH: Sideway! What are you doing?

SIDEWAY: I'm checking that you're safe and sound returned. That's what the line says: 'Safe and sound returned.'

RALPH: You don't need to touch him. You can see that!

SIDEWAY: Yes, yes. I'll check his different parts with my eyes. Now, I'll put it all together, 'Plume! My dear Captain, welcome. Safe and sound returned!'

He does this with appropriate gestures.

RALPH: Sideway – it's a very good attempt. It's very theatrical. But you could try to be a little more-euh-natural.

SIDEWAY: Natural! On the stage! But Mr Clark!

RALPH: People must -euh-believe you. Garrick after all is admired for his naturalness.

SIDEWAY: Of course. I thought I was being Garrick - but never mind. Natural. Quite. You're the director, Mr Clark.

RALPH: Perhaps you could look at me while you're saying the lines.

SIDEWAY: But the audience won't see my face.

RALPH: The lines are said to Captain Plume. Let's move on. Plume says: 'I 'scaped safe from Germany', shall we say – America? It will make it more contemporary –

WISEHAMMER: You can't change the words of the playwright.

RALPH: Mm, well, 'and sound, I hope, from London: you see I have –'

BLACK CAESAR *rushes on.*

RALPH: Caesar, we're rehearsing - would you –

CAESAR: I see that well, Monsieur Lieutenant. I see it is a piece of theatre, I have seen many pieces of theatre in my

beautiful island of Madagascar so I have decided to play in your piece of theatre.

RALPH: There's no part for you.

CAESAR: There is always a part for Caesar.

SIDEWAY: All the parts have been taken.

CAESAR: I will play his servant.

He stands next to SIDEWAY.

RALPH: Farquhar hasn't written a servant for Worthy.

DUCKLING: He can have my part. I want to play something else.

CAESAR: There is always a black servant in a play, Monsieur Lieutenant. And Caesar is that servant. So, now I stand here just behind him and I will be his servant.

RALPH: There are no lines for it, Caesar.

CAESAR: I speak in French. That makes him a more high up gentleman if he has a French servant, and that is good. Now he gets the lady with the black servant. Very chic.

RALPH: I'll think about it. Actually, I would like to rehearse the ladies now. They have been waiting patiently and we don't have much time left. Freeman, would you go and see what's happened to Arscott. Sideway, we'll come back to this scene another time, but that was very good, very good. A little, a little euh, but very good.

SIDEWAY *bows out, followed by* CAESAR.

RALPH: Now we will rehearse the first scene between Melinda and Silvia. Morden and Brenham, if you would come and stand here. Now the scene is set in Melinda's apartments. Silvia is already there. So, if you stand here, Morden. Brenham, you stand facing her.

LIZ (*very, very fast*): 'Welcome to town cousin Silvia I envied you your retreat in the country for Shrewsbury methinks and all your heads of shires are the most irregular places for living' –

RALPH: Euh, Morden –

LIZ: Wait, I haven't finished yet. 'Here we have smoke noise scandal affectation and pretension in short everything to give the spleen and nothing to divert it then the air is intolerable' –

RALPH: Morden, you know the lines very well.

LIZ: Thank you, Lieutenant Clark.

RALPH: But you might want to try and act them.

Pause.

Let's look at the scene.

LIZ *looks.*

RALPH: You're a rich lady. You're at home. Now a rich lady would stand in a certain way. Try to stand like a rich lady. Try to look at Silvia with a certain assurance.

LIZ: Assurance.

WISEHAMMER: Confidence.

RALPH: Like this. You've seen rich ladies, haven't you?

LIZ: I robbed a few.

RALPH: How did they behave?

LIZ: They screamed.

RALPH: I mean before you-euh-robbed them.

LIZ: I don't know. I was watching their purses.

RALPH: Have you ever seen a lady in her own house?

LIZ: I used to climb into the big houses when I was a girl, and just stand there, looking. I didn't take anything. I just stood. Like this.

RALPH: But if it was your own house, you would think it was normal to live like that.

WISEHAMMER: It's not normal. It's not normal when others have nothing.

RALPH: When acting, you have to imagine things. You have to imagine you're someone different. So, now, think of a rich lady and imagine you're her.

LIZ *begins to masticate.*

RALPH: What are you doing?

LIZ: If I was rich I'd eat myself sick.

DABBY: Me too, potatoes.

The convicts speak quickly and over each other.

SIDEWAY: Roast beef and Yorkshire pudding.

CAESAR: Hearts of palm.

WISEHAMMER: Four fried eggs, six fried eggs, eight fried eggs.

LIZ: Eels, oysters –

RALPH: Could we get on with the scene, please? Brenham, it's your turn to speak.

MARY: 'Oh, madam, I have heard the town commended for its air.'

LIZ: 'But you don't consider Silvia how long I have lived in't!'

RALPH (*to* LIZ): I believe you would look at her.

LIZ: She didn't look at me.

RALPH: Didn't she? She will now.

LIZ: 'For I can assure you that to a lady the least nice in her constitution no air can be good above half a year change of air I take to be the most agreeable of any variety in life.'

MARY: 'But prithee, my dear Melinda, don't put on such an air to me.'

RALPH: Excellent, Brenham. You could be a little more sharp on the 'don't'.

MARY: 'Don't.' (MARY *now tries a few gestures.*) 'Your education and mine were just the same, and I remember the time when we never troubled our heads about air, but when the sharp air from the Welsh mountains made our noses drop in a cold morning at the boarding-school.'

RALPH: Good! Good! Morden?

LIZ: 'Our education cousin was the same but our temperaments had nothing alike.'

RALPH: That's a little better, Morden, but you needn't be quite so angry with her. Now go on Brenham.

LIZ: I haven't finished my speech!

RALPH: You're right, Morden, please excuse me.

LIZ: No, no, there's no need for that, Lieutenant. I only meant – I don't have to

RALPH: Please do.

LIZ: 'You have the constitution of a horse.'

RALPH: Much better, Morden. But you must always remember you're a lady. What can we do to help you? Lucy.

DABBY: That's you, Duckling.

RALPH: See that little piece of wood over there? Take it to Melinda. That will be your fan.

DUCKLING: I'm not fetching nothing for Liz.

RALPH: She's not Morden, she's Melinda, your mistress. You're her servant, Lucy. In fact, you should be in this scene. Now take her that fan.

DUCKLING (*gives the wood to* LIZ): Here.

LIZ: Thank you, Lucy, I do much appreciate your effort.

RALPH: No, you would nod your head.

WISEHAMMER: Don't add any words to the play.

RALPH: Now, Lucy, stand behind Morden.

DUCKLING: What do I say?

RALPH: Nothing.

DUCKLING: How will they know I'm here? Why does she get all the lines? Why can't I have some of hers?

RALPH: Brenham, it's your speech.

MARY: 'So far as to be troubled with neither spleen, colic, nor vapours' –

The convicts slink away and sink down, trying to make themselves invisible as MAJOR ROSS, *followed by* CAPTAIN CAMPBELL *come on.*

MARY: I need no salt for my stomach, no –

She sees the officers herself and folds in with the rest of the convicts.

RALPH: Major Ross, Captain Campbell, I'm rehearsing.

ROSS: Rehearsing! Rehearsing!

CAMPBELL: Tssaach. Rehearsing.

ROSS: Lieutenant Clark is rehearsing. Lieutenant Clark asked us to give the prisoners two hours so he could rehearse, but what has he done with them? What?

CAMPBELL: Eeeh. Other things, eh.

ROSS: Where are the prisoners Kable and Arscott, Lieutenant?

CAMPBELL: Eh?

RALPH: They seem to be late.

ROSS: While you were rehearsing, Arscott and Kable slipped into the woods with three others, so five men have run away and it's all because of your damned play and your so-called thespists. And not only have your thespists run away, they've stolen food from the stores for their renegade escapade, that's what your play has done.

RALPH: I don't see what the play –

ROSS: I said it from the beginning. The play will bring down calamity on this colony.

RALPH: I don't see –

ROSS: The devil, Lieutenant, always comes through the mind, here, worms its way, idleness and words.

RALPH: Major Ross, I can't agree –

ROSS: Listen to me, my lad, you're a second lieutenant and you don't agree or disagree with Major Ross.

CAMPBELL: No discipline, tcchhha.

ROSS *looks over the convicts.*

ROSS: Caesar! He started going with them and came back.

RALPH: That's all right, he's not in the play.

CAESAR: Yes I am, please Lieutenant, I am a servant.

ROSS: John Wisehammer!

WISEHAMMER: I had nothing to do with it!

ROSS: You're Jewish, aren't you? You're guilty. Kable was last seen near Wisehammer's hut. Liz Morden! She was observed next to the colony's stores late last night in the company of Kable who was supposed to be repairing the door. (*To* LIZ.) Liz Morden, you will be tried for stealing from the stores. You know the punishment? Death by hanging. And now you may continue to rehearse, Lieutenant.

ROSS *goes.* *CAMPBELL* *lingers, looking at the book.*

CAMPBELL: Ouusstta. 'The Recruiting Officer'. Good title. Arara. But a play, tss, a play.

He goes. RALPH *and the convicts are left in the shambles of their rehearsal. A silence.*

ACT TWO

Scene One

Visiting Hours

LIZ, WISEHAMMER, ARSCOTT, CAESAR *all in chains.* ARSCOTT *is bent over, facing away.*

LIZ: Luck? Don't know the word. Shifts its bob when I comes near. Born under a ha'penny planet I was. Dad's a nibbler, don't want to get crapped. Mum leaves. Five brothers, I'm the only titter. I takes in washing. Then. My own father. Lady's walking down the street, takes her wiper. She screams, he's shoulder-clapped, says, it's not me, Sir, it's Lizzie, look, she took it. I'm stripped, beaten in the street, everyone watching. That night, I take my dad's cudgel and try to kill him, I prig all his clothes and go to my older brother. He don't want me. Liz, he says, why trine for a make, when you can wap for a winne? I'm no dimber mort, I says. Don't ask you to be a swell mollisher, Sister, men want Miss Laycock, don't look at your mug. So I begin to sell my mother of saints. I thinks I'm in luck when I meet the swell cove. He's a bobcull. He says to me, it's not enough to sell your mossie face, Lizzie, it don't bring no shiners no more. Shows me how to spice the swells. So. Swell has me up the wall, flashes a pocket watch, I lifts it. But one time I stir my stumps too slow, the swell squeaks beef, the snoozie hears, I'm nibbed. It's up the ladder to rest, I thinks when I goes up before the fortune teller, but no, the judge's a bobcull, I nap the King's pardon and it's seven years across the herring pond. Jesus Christ the hunger on the ship, sailors won't touch me: no rantum scantum, no food, but here, the Governor says, new life. You could nob it here, Lizzie, I thinks, bobcull gov, this niffynaffy play, not too much work, good crew of rufflers, Kable, Arscott, but no, Ross don't like my mug, I'm nibbed again and now it's up the ladder to rest for good. Well. Lizzie Morden's life. And you, Wisehammer, how did you get here?

WISEHAMMER: Betrayal. Barbarous falsehood. Intimidation: injustice.

LIZ: Speak in English, Wisehammer.

WISEHAMMER: I am innocent. I didn't do it and I'll keep saying I didn't.

LIZ: It doesn't matter what you say. If they say you're a thief, you're a thief.

WISEHAMMER: I am not a thief. I'll go back to England to the snuff shop of Rickett and Loads and say, see, I'm back, I'm innocent.

LIZ: They won't listen.

WISEHAMMER: You can't live if you think that way.

Pause.

I'm sorry. Seven years and I'll go back.

LIZ: What do you want to go back to England for? You're not English.

WISEHAMMER: I was born in England. I'm English. What do I have to do to make people believe I'm English?

LIZ: You have to think English. I hate England. But I think English. And him, Arscott, he's not said anything, since they brought him in but he's thinking English, I can tell.

CAESAR: I don't want to think English. If I think English I will die. I want to go back to Madagascar and think Malagasy. I want to die in Madagascar and join my ancestors.

LIZ: It doesn't matter where you die when you're dead.

CAESAR: If I die here, I will have no spirit. I want to go home. I will escape again.

ARSCOTT: There's no escape from here.

CAESAR: This time I lost my courage, but next time I ask my ancestors and they will help me escape.

ARSCOTT (*shouts*): There's no escape!

LIZ: See. That's English. You know things.

CAESAR: My ancestors will know the way.

ARSCOTT: There's no escape I tell you.

Pause.

You go in circles out there, that's all you do. You go out there and you walk and walk and you don't reach China you come back on your steps if the savages don't get you first. Even a compass doesn't work in this foreign upside-down desert. Here. You can read. Why didn't it work? What does it say?

He hands WISEHAMMER *a carefully folded, wrinkled piece of paper.*

WISEHAMMER: It says North.

ARSCOTT: Why didn't it work then? It was supposed to take us north to China, why did I end up going in circles?

WISEHAMMER: Because it's not a compass.

ARSCOTT: I gave my only shilling to a sailor for it. He said it was a compass.

WISEHAMMER: It's a piece of paper with north written on it. He lied. He deceived you, he betrayed you.

SIDEWAY, MARY *and* DUCKLING *come on.*

SIDEWAY: Madam, gentlemen, fellow players, we have come to visit, to commiserate, to offer our humble services.

LIZ: Get out!

MARY: Liz, we've come to rehearse the play.

WISEHAMMER: Rehearse the play?

DUCKLING: The Lieutenant has gone to talk to the Governor. Harry said we could come see you.

MARY: The Lieutenant has asked me to stand in his place so we don't lose time. We'll start with the first scene between Melinda and Brazen.

WISEHAMMER: How can I play Captain Brazen in chains?

MARY: This is the theatre. We will believe you.

ARSCOTT: Where does Kite come in?

SIDEWAY (*bowing to* LIZ): Madam, I have brought you your fan.

Scene Two

His Excellency Exhorts Ralph

PHILLIP, RALPH.

PHILLIP: I hear you want to stop the play, Lieutenant.

RALPH: Half of my cast is in chains, Sir.

PHILLIP: That is a difficulty, but it can be overcome. Is that your only reason, Lieutenant?

RALPH: So many people seem against it, Sir.

PHILLIP: Are you afraid?

RALPH: No, Sir, but I do not wish to displease my superior officers.

PHILLIP: If you break conventions, it's inevitable you make enemies, Lieutenant. This play irritates them.

RALPH: Yes and I –

PHILLIP: Socrates irritated the state of Athens and was put to death for it.

RALPH: Sir –

PHILLIP: Would you have a world without Socrates?

RALPH: Sir, I –

PHILLIP: In the Meno, one of Plato's great dialogues, have you read it, Lieutenant, Socrates demonstrates that a slave boy can learn the principles of geometry as well as a gentleman.

RALPH: Ah –

PHILLIP: In other words, he shows that human beings have an intelligence which has nothing to do with the circumstances into which they are born.

RALPH: Sir –

PHILLIP: Sit down, Lieutenant. It is a matter of reminding the slave of what he knows, of his own intelligence. And by intelligence you may read goodness, talent, the innate qualities of human beings.

RALPH: I see – Sir.

PHILLIP: When he treats the slave boy as a rational human being, the boy becomes one, he loses his fear, and he becomes a competent mathematician. A little more encouragement and he might become an extraordinary mathematician. Who knows? You must see your actors in that light.

RALPH: I can see some of them, Sir, but there are others . . . John Arscott –

PHILLIP: He has been given 200 lashes for trying to escape. It will take time for him to see himself as a human being again.

RALPH: Liz Morden –

PHILLIP: Liz Morden – (*He pauses.*) I had a

reason for asking you to cast her as Melinda. Morden is one of the most difficult women in the colony.

RALPH: She is indeed, Sir.

PHILLIP: Lower than a slave, full of loathing, foul mouthed, desperate.

RALPH: Exactly, Sir. And violent.

PHILLIP: Quite. To be made an example of.

RALPH: By hanging?

PHILLIP: No, Lieutenant, by redemption.

RALPH: The Reverend says he's given up on her, Sir.

PHILLIP: The Reverend's an ass, Lieutenant. I am speaking of redeeming her humanity.

RALPH: I am afraid there may not be much there, Sir.

PHILLIP: How do we know what humanity lies hidden under the rags and filth of a mangled life? I have seen soldiers given up for dead, limbs torn, heads cut open, come back to life. If we treat her as a corpse, of course she will die. Try a little kindness, Lieutenant.

RALPH: But will she be hanged, Sir?

PHILLIP: I don't want a woman to be hanged. You will have to help, Ralph.

RALPH: Sir!

PHILLIP: I had retired from His Majesty's Service, Ralph. I was farming. I don't know why they asked me to rule over this colony of wretched souls, but I will fulfil my responsibility. No one will stop me.

RALPH: No, Sir, but I don't see –

PHILLIP: What is a statesman's responsibility? To ensure the rule of law. But the citizens must be taught to obey that law of their own will. I want to rule over responsible human beings, not tyrannise over a group of animals. I want there to be a contract between us, not a whip on my side, terror and hatred on theirs. And you must help me, Ralph.

RALPH: Yes, Sir. The play –

PHILLIP: Won't change much, but it is the diagram in the sand that may remind – just remind the slave boy – Do you understand?

RALPH: I think so.

PHILLIP: We may fail. I may have a mutiny

on my hands. They are trying to convince the admiralty that I am mad.

RALPH: Sir!

PHILLIP: And they will threaten you. You don't want to be a second lieutenant all your life.

RALPH: No, Sir.

PHILLIP: I cannot go over the head of Major Ross in the matter of promotion.

RALPH: I see.

PHILLIP: But we have embarked, Ralph, we must stay afloat. There is a more serious threat and it may capsize us all. If a ship does not come within three months, the supplies will be exhausted. In a month, I will cut the rations again. (*Pause.*) Harry is not well. Can you do something? Good luck with the play, Lieutenant. Oh, and Ralph –

RALPH: Sir –

PHILLIP: Unexpected situations are often matched by unexpected virtue in people, are they not?

RALPH: I believe they are, Sir.

PHILLIP: A play is a world in itself, a tiny colony we could almost say.

Pause.

And you are in charge of it. That is a great responsibility.

RALPH: I will lay down my life if I have to, Sir.

PHILLIP: I don't think it will come to that, Lieutenant. You need only do your best.

RALPH: Yes, Sir, I will, Sir.

PHILLIP: Excellent.

RALPH: It's a wonderful play, Sir. I wasn't sure at first, as you know, but now –

PHILLIP: Good, Good. I shall look forward to seeing it. I'm sure it will be a success.

RALPH: Thank you, Sir. Thank you.

Scene Three

Harry Brewer Sees the Dead

HARRY BREWER's *tent. HARRY sits, drinking rum, speaking in the different*

*voices of his tormenting ghosts and
answering in his own.*

HARRY: Duckling! Duckling! 'She's on the
beach, Harry, waiting for her young Handy
Baker.' Go away, Handy, go away! 'The
dead never go away, Harry. You thought
you'd be the only one to dance the buttock
ball with your trull, but no one owns a
whore's cunt, Harry, you rent.' I didn't
hang you. 'You wanted me dead.' I didn't.

'You wanted me hanged.' All right, I
wanted you hanged, Go away! 'Death is
horrible, Mr Brewer, it's dark, there's
nothing.' Thomas Barrett! You were
hanged because you stole from the stores.
'I was 17, Mr Brewer.' You lived a very
wicked life. 'I didn't.' That's what you
said that morning, 'I have led a very
wicked life'. 'I had to say something, Mr
Brewer, and make sense of dying. I'd
heard the Reverend say we were all
wicked, but it was horrible, my body
hanging, my tongue sticking out.' You
shouldn't have stolen that food! 'I wanted
to live, go back to England, I'd only be 24.
I hadn't done it much, not like you.'
Duckling! 'I wish I wasn't dead, Mr
Brewer I had plans. I was going to have my
farm, drink with friends and feel the strong
legs of a girl around me –' You shouldn't
have stolen. 'Didn't you ever steal?' No!
Yes. But that was different. Duckling!
'Why should you be alive after what
you've done?' Duckling! Duckling!

DUCKLING *rushes on.*

DUCKLING: What's the matter, Harry?

HARRY: I'm seeing them.

DUCKLING: Who?

HARRY: All of them. The dead. Help me.

DUCKLING: I heard your screams from the
beach. You're having another bad dream.

HARRY: No. I see them.

Pause

Let me come inside you.

DUCKLING: Now?

HARRY: Please.

DUCKLING: Will you forget your
nightmares?

HARRY: Yes.

DUCKLING: Come then.

HARRY: Duckling . . .

Pause.

What were you doing on the beach? You
were with him, he told me, you were with
Handy Baker.

Scene Four

The Aborigine muses on the nature of dreams

THE ABORIGINE: Some dreams lose their
way and wander over the earth, lost. But
this is a dream no one wants. It has stayed.
How can we befriend this crowded,
hungry and disturbed dream?

Scene Five

The Second Rehearsal

RALPH CLARK, MARY BRENHAM *and*
ROBERT SIDEWAY *are waiting.* MAJOR
ROSS *and* CAPTAIN CAMPBELL *bring
the three prisoners* CAESAR,
WISEHAMMER *and* LIZ MORDEN. *They
are still in chains.* ROSS *shoves them
forward.*

ROSS: Here is some of your caterwauling
cast, Lieutenant.

CAMPBELL: The Governor, chhht, said,
release, tssst. Prisoners.

ROSS: Unchain Wisehammer and the
Savage, Captain Campbell. (*Points to*
LIZ.) She stays in chains. She's being tried
tomorrow, we don't want her sloping off.

RALPH: I can't rehearse with one of my
players in chains, Major.

CAMPBELL: Eeh. Difficult. Mmmm.

ROSS: We'll tell the Governor you didn't
need her and take her back to prison.

RALPH: No. We shall manage. Sideway, go
over the scene you rehearsed in prison
with Melinda, please.

CAESAR: I'm in that scene too, Lieutenant.

RALPH: No you're not.

LIZ and SIDEWAY: Yes he is, Lieutenant.

SIDEWAY: He's my servant.

RALPH *nods and* LIZ, SIDEWAY *and* CAESAR *move to the side and stand together, ready to rehearse, but waiting.*

RALPH: The rest of us will go from Silvia's entrance as Wilful. Where's Arscott?

ROSS: We haven't finished with Arscott yet, Lieutenant.

CAMPBELL: Punishment, eeeh, for escape. Fainted. 53 lashes left. Heeeh.

ROSS (*pointing to* CAESAR): Caesar's next. After Morden's trial.

CAESAR *cringes.*

RALPH: Brenham, are you ready? Wisehammer? I'll play Captain Plume.

ROSS: The wee Lieutenant wants to be in the play too. He wants to be promoted to convict. We'll have you in the chain gang soon, Mr Clark, haha.

RALPH: Major, we will rehearse now.

Pause. No one moves.

We wish to rehearse.

ROSS: No one's stopping you, Lieutenant.

Silence.

RALPH: Major, rehearsals need to take place in the utmost euh – privacy, secrecy you might say. The actors are not yet ready to be seen by the public.

ROSS: Not ready to be seen?

RALPH: Major, there is a modesty attached to the process of creation which must be respected.

ROSS: Modesty? Modesty! Sideway, come here.

RALPH: Major. Sideway – stay –

ROSS: Lieutenant, I would not try to countermand the orders of a superior officer.

CAMPBELL: Obedience. Ehh. First euh, rule.

ROSS: Sideway.

SIDEWAY *comes up to* ROSS.

ROSS: Take your shirt off.

SIDEWAY *obeys.* ROSS *turns him and shows his scarred back to the company.*

One hundred lashes on the Sirius for answering an officer. Remember, Sideway? Three hundred lashes for trying to strike the same officer.

I have seen the white of this animal's bones, his wretched blood and reeky convict urine have spilled on my boots and he's feeling modest? Are you feeling modest, Sideway?

He shoves SIDEWAY *aside.*

Modesty.

Bryant. Here.

DABBY *comes forward.*

On your knees.

DABBY *obeys.*

On all fours.

DABBY *goes down on all fours.*

Now wag your tail and bark, and I'll throw you a biscuit. What? You've forgotten? Isn't that how you begged for your food on the ship? Wag your tail, Bryant, bark! We'll wait.
    Brenham.

MARY *comes forward.*

Where's your tattoo, Brenham? Show us. I can't see it. Show us.

MARY *tries to obey, lifting her skirt a little.*

If you can't manage, I'll help you. (MARY *lifts her skirt a little higher.*) I can't see it.

But SIDEWAY *turns to* LIZ *and starts acting, boldly, across the room, across everyone.*

SIDEWAY: 'What pleasures I may receive abroad are indeed uncertain; but this I am sure of, I shall meet with less cruelty among the most barbarous nations than I have found at home.'

LIZ: 'Come, Sir, you and I have been jangling a great while; I fancy if we made up our accounts, we should the sooner come to an agreement.'

SIDEWAY: 'Sure, Madam, you won't dispute your being in my debt – my fears, sighs, vows, promises, assiduities, anxieties, jealousies, have run on for a whole year, without any payment.'

CAMPBELL: Mmhem, good, that. Sighs, vows, promises, hehem, mmm. Anxieties.

ROSS: Captain Campbell, start Arscott's punishment.

CAMPBELL *goes.*

LIZ: 'A year! Oh Mr Worthy, what you owe to me is not to be paid under a seven years' servitude. How did you use me the year before –'

The shouts of ARSCOTT *are heard.*

'How did you use me the year before' –

She loses her lines. SIDEWAY *tries to prompt her.*

SIDEWAY: 'When taking advantage –'

LIZ: 'When taking the advantage of my innocence and necessity' –

But she stops and drops down, defeated. Silence, except for the beating and ARSCOTT'*s cries.*

Scene Six

The Science of Hanging

HARRY, KETCH FREEMAN, LIZ, *sitting, staring straight ahead of her.*

KETCH: I don't want to do this.

HARRY: Get on with it, Freeman.

KETCH (*to* LIZ): I have to measure you.

Pause.

I'm sorry.

LIZ *doesn't move.*

You'll have to stand, Liz.

LIZ *doesn't move.*

Please.

Pause.

I won't hurt you. I mean, now. And if I

have the measurements right, I can make it quick. Very quick. Please.

LIZ *doesn't move.*

She doesn't want to get up, Mr Brewer. I could come back later.

HARRY: Hurry up.

KETCH: I can't. I can't measure her unless she gets up.
      I have to measure her to judge the drop. If the rope's too short, it won't hang her and if the rope is too long, it could pull her head off. It's very difficult, Mr Brewer, I've always done my best.

Pause.

But I've never hung a woman.

HARRY: 'You've hung a boy.' (*To* KETCH.) You've hung a boy.

KETCH: That was a terrible mess, Mr Brewer, don't you remember. It took twenty minutes and even then he wasn't dead. Remember how he danced and everyone laughed. I don't want to repeat something like that, Mr Brewer, not now. Someone had to get hold of his legs to weigh him down and then –

HARRY: Measure her, Freeman!

KETCH: Yes, Sir. Could you tell her to get up. She'll listen to you.

HARRY (*shouts*): Get up, you bitch.

LIZ *doesn't move.*

HARRY: Get up!

He seizes her.

Now measure her!

KETCH (*measuring the neck, etc of* LIZ): The Lieutenant is talking to the Governor again, Liz, maybe he'll change his mind. At least he might wait until we've done the play.

Pause.

I don't want to do this.

I know, you're thinking in my place you wouldn't. But somebody will do it, if I don't, and I'll be gentle. I won't hurt you.

LIZ *doesn't move, doesn't look at him.*

It's wrong, Mr Brewer. It's wrong.

HARRY (*in* TOM BARRETT's *voice*): 'It's wrong. Death is horrible.' (*In his own voice to* KETCH.) There's no food left in the colony and she steals it and gives it to Kable to run away.

KETCH: That's true, Liz, you shouldn't have stolen that food. Especially when the Lieutenant trusted us. That was wrong, Liz. Still, I'm sorry. I'll do my best.

HARRY: 'I had plans.' (*To* KETCH.) Are you finished?

KETCH: Yes, yes. I have all the measurements I need. No, one more. I need to lift her. You don't mind, do you, Liz?

He lifts her.

KETCH: She's so light. I'll have to use a very long rope. The fig tree would be better, it's higher. When will they build me some gallows, Mr Brewer? Nobody will laugh at you, Liz, you won't be shamed, I'll make sure of that.

HARRY: 'You could hang yourself.' Come on, Freeman. Let's go.

KETCH: Goodbye, Liz. You were a very good Melinda. No one will be as good as you.

They begin to go.

LIZ: Mr Brewer.

HARRY: 'You wanted me dead.' I didn't. You shouldn't've stolen that food!

KETCH: Speak to her, please, Mr Brewer.

HARRY: What?

LIZ: Tell Lieutenant Clark I didn't steal the food. Tell him – afterwards. I want him to know.

HARRY: Why didn't you say that before? Why are you lying now?

LIZ: Tell the Lieutenant.

HARRY: 'Another victim of yours, another body. I was so frightened, so alone.'

KETCH: Mr Brewer.

HARRY: 'It's dark. There's nothing.' Get away, get away!

LIZ: Please tell the Lieutenant.

HARRY: First fear, then a pain at the back of the neck. Then nothing. I can't see. It's dark. It's dark.

HARRY *screams and falls.*

Scene Seven

The Meaning of Plays

THE ABORIGINE: Ghosts in a multitude have spilled from the dream. Who are they? A swarm of ancestors comes through unmended cracks in the sky. But why? What do they need? If we can satisfy them, they will go back. How can we satisfy them?

MARY, RALPH, DABBY, WISEHAMMER, ARSCOTT. MARY *and* RALPH *are rehearsing. The others are watching.*

RALPH: 'For I swear, madam, by the honour of my profession, that whatever dangers I went upon, it was with the hope of making myself more worthy of your esteem, and if I ever had thoughts of preserving my life, 'twas for the pleasure of dying at your feet.'

MARY: 'Well, well, you shall die at my feet, or where you will; but you know, sir, there is a certain will and testament to be made beforehand.'

I don't understand why Silvia has asked Plume to make a will.

DABBY: It's a proof of his love, he wants to provide for her.

MARY: A will is a proof of love?

WISEHAMMER: No. She's using will in another sense. He must show his willingness to marry her. Dying is used in another sense, too.

RALPH: He gives her his will to indicate that he intends to take care of her.

DABBY: That's right, Lieutenant, marriage is nothing, but will you look after her?

WISEHAMMER: Plume is too ambitious to marry Silvia.

MARY: If I had been Silvia, I would have

trusted Plume.

DABBY: When dealing with men, always have a contract.

MARY: Love is a contract.

DABBY: Love is the barter of perishable goods. A man's word for a woman's body.

WISEHAMMER: Dabby is right. If a man loves a woman, he should marry her.

RALPH: Sometimes he can't.

WISEHAMMER: Then she should look for someone who can.

DABBY: A woman should look after her own interests, that's all.

MARY: Her interest is to love.

DABBY: A girl will love the first man who knows how to open her legs. She's called a whore and ends up here. I could write scenes, Lieutenant, women with real lives, not these Shrewsbury prudes.

WISEHAMMER: I've written something. The prologue of this play won't make any sense to the convicts: 'In ancient times, when Helen's fatal charms' and so on – I've written another one. Will you look at it, Lieutenant?

RALPH *does so and* WISEHAMMER *takes* MARY *aside.*

You mustn't trust the wrong people, Mary. We could make a new life together, here. I would marry you, Mary, think about it, you would live with me, in a house. He'll have to put you in a hut at the bottom of his garden and call you his servant in public, that is, his whore. Don't do it, Mary.

DABBY: Lieutenant, are we rehearsing or not? Arscott and I have been waiting for hours.

RALPH: It seems interesting, I'll read it more carefully later.

WISEHAMMER: You don't like it.

RALPH: I do like it. Perhaps it needs a little more work. It's not Farquhar.

WISEHAMMER: It would mean more to the convicts.

RALPH: We'll talk about it another time.

WISEHAMMER: Do you think it should be longer?

RALPH: I'll think about it.

WISEHAMMER: Shorter? Do you like the last two lines. Mary helped me with them.

RALPH: Ah.

WISEHAMMER: The first lines took us days, didn't they, Mary?

RALPH: We'll rehearse Silvia's entrance as Jack Wilful. You're in the scene, Wisehammer. We'll come to your scenes in a minute, Bryant. Now, Brenham, remember what I showed you yesterday about walking like a gentleman? I've ordered britches to be made for you, you can practise in them tomorrow.

MARY: I'll tuck my skirt in. (*She does so and takes a masculine pose.*) 'Save ye, save ye, gentlemen.'

WISEHAMMER: 'My dear, I'm yours.'

He kisses her.

RALPH: It doesn't say Silvia is kissed in the stage directions.

WISEHAMMER: Plume kisses her later and there's the line about men kissing in the army, I thought Brazen would kiss her immediately.

RALPH: It's completely wrong.

WISEHAMMER: It's right for the character of Brazen.

RALPH: No it isn't. I'm the director, Wisehammer.

WISEHAMMER: Yes, but I have to play the part. They're equal in this scene. They're both captains and in the end fight for her. Who's playing Plume in our performance?

RALPH: I will have to, as Kable hasn't come back. It's your line.

WISEHAMMER: 'No, but I will presently. Your name, my dear?' Will I be given a sword?

RALPH: I doubt it. Let's move onto Kite's entrance, Arscott has been waiting too long.

ARSCOTT (*delighted, launches straight in*): 'Sir, if you please' –

RALPH: Excellent, Arscott, but we should just give you our last lines so you'll know when to come in. Wisehammer.

WISEHAMMER: 'The fellow dare not fight.'

RALPH: That's when you come in.

ARSCOTT: 'Sir, if you please' –

DABBY: What about me? I haven't done anything either. You always rehearse the scenes with Silvia.

RALPH: Let's rehearse the scene where Rose comes on with her brother Bullock. It's a better scene for you Arscott. Do you know it?

ARSCOTT: Yes.

RALPH: Good. Wisehammer, you'll have to play the part of Bullock.

WISEHAMMER: What? Play two parts?

RALPH: Major Ross won't let any more prisoners off work. Some of you will have to play several parts.

WISEHAMMER: It'll confuse the audience. They'll think Brazen is Bullock and Bullock Brazen.

RALPH: Nonsense, if the audience is paying attention, they'll know that Bullock is a country boy and Brazen a captain.

WISEHAMMER: What if they aren't paying attention?

RALPH: People who can't pay attention should not go to the theatre.

MARY: If you act well, they will have to pay attention.

WISEHAMMER: It will ruin my entrance as Captain Brazen.

RALPH: We have no choice and we must turn this necessity into an advantage. You will play two very different characters and display the full range of your abilities.

WISEHAMMER: Our audience won't be that discerning.

RALPH: Their imagination will be challenged and trained. Let's start the scene. Bryant?

DABBY: I think 'The Recruiting Officer' is a silly play. I want to be in a play that has more interesting people in it.

MARY: I like playing Silvia. She's bold, she breaks rules out of love for her Captain and she's not ashamed.

DABBY: She hasn't been born poor, she hasn't had to survive, and her father's a Justice of the Peace. I want to play myself.

ARSCOTT: I don't want to play myself. When I say Kite's lines I forget everything else. I forget the judge said I'm going to have to spend the rest of my natural life in this place getting beaten and working like a slave. I can forget that out there it's trees and burnt grass, spiders that kill you in four hours and snakes. I don't have to think about what happened to Kable, I don't have to remember the things I've done, when I speak Kite's lines I don't hate anymore. I'm Kite, I'm in Shrewsbury. Can we get on with the scene, Lieutenant, and stop talking?

DABBY: I want to see a play that shows life as we know it.

WISEHAMMER: A play should make you understand something new. If it tells you what you already know, you leave it as ignorant as you went in.

DABBY: Why can't we do a play about now?

WISEHAMMER: It doesn't matter when a play is set. It's better if it's set in the past, it's clearer. It's easier to understand Plume and Brazen than some of the officers we know here.

RALPH: Arscott, would you start the scene?

ARSCOTT: 'Captain, Sir, look yonder, a-coming this way, 'tis the prettiest, cleanest, little tit.'

RALPH: Now Worthy – He's in this scene. Where's Sideway?

MARY: He's so upset about Liz he won't rehearse.

RALPH: I am going to talk to the Governor, but he has to rehearse. We must do the play, whatever happens. We've been rehearsing for five months! Let's go on. 'Here she comes, and what is that great country fellow with her?'

ARSCOTT: 'I can't tell, Sir.'

WISEHAMMER: I'm not a great country fellow.

RALPH: Act it, Wisehammer.

DABBY: 'Buy chickens, young and tender, young and tender chickens.' This is a very stupid line and I'm not saying it.

RALPH: It's written by the playwright and you have to say it. 'Here, you chickens!'

DABBY: 'Who calls?'

RALPH: Bryant, you're playing a pretty country wench who wants to entice the Captain. You have to say these lines with charm and euh – blushes.

DABBY: I don't blush.

RALPH: I can't do this scene without Sideway. Let's do another scene.

Pause.

Arscott, let's work on your big speeches, I haven't heard them yet. I still need Sideway. This is irresponsible, he wanted the part. Somebody go and get Sideway.

No one moves.

ARSCOTT: I'll do the first speech anyway, Sir.

'Yes, Sir, I understand my business, I will say it; you must know, Sir, I was born a gypsy, and bred among that crew till I was ten year old, there I learned canting and lying;' –

DABBY: That's about me!

ARSCOTT: 'I was bought from my mother Cleopatra by a certain nobleman, for three guineas, who liking my beauty made me his page ' –

DABBY: That's my story. Why do I have to play a silly milkmaid? Why can't I play Kite?

MARY: You can't play a man, Dabby.

DABBY: You're playing a man: Jack Wilful.

MARY: Yes, but in the play, I know I'm a woman, whereas if you played Kite, you would have to think you were a man.

DABBY: If Wisehammer can think he's a big country lad, I can think I'm a man. People will use their imagination and people with no imagination shouldn't go to the theatre.

RALPH: Bryant, you're muddling everything.

DABBY: No. I see things very clearly and I'm making you see clearly, Lieutenant. I want to play Kite.

ARSCOTT: You can't play Kite! I'm playing Kite! You can't steal my part!

RALPH: You may have to play Melinda.

DABBY: All she does is marry Sideway, that's not interesting.

DABBY *stomps off.*

KETCH *comes on.*

KETCH: I'm sorry I'm late, Lieutenant, but I know all my lines.

RALPH: We'll rehearse the first scene between Justice Balance and Silvia. Brenham.

ARSCOTT *stomps off.*

MARY: 'Whilst there is life there is hope, sir; perhaps my brother may recover.'

KETCH: 'We have but little reason to expect it –'

MARY: I can't. Not with him. Not with Liz – I can't.

She runs off.

RALPH: One has to transcend personal feelings in the theatre.

WISEHAMMER *runs after* MARY.

We're not making much progress today, let's end this rehearsal.

He goes. KETCH *is left alone, bewildered.*

Scene Eight
Duckling Makes Vows

Night. HARRY, *ill.* DUCKLING.

DUCKLING: If you live, I will never again punish you with my silence. If you live, I will never again turn away from you. If you live, I will never again imagine another man when you make love to me. If you live, I will never tell you I want to leave you. If you live, I will speak to you. If you live, I will be tender with you. If you live, I will look after you. If you live, I will stay with you. If you live, I will be wet and open to your touch. If you live, I will answer all your questions. If you live, I will look at you. If you live, I will love you.

Pause.

If you die, I will never forgive you.

She leans over him. Listens. Touches. HARRY *is dead.*

I hate you.

No. I love you.

She crumples into a foetal position, cries out.

How could you do this?

Scene Nine

A Love Scene

The beach. Night. MARY, *then* RALPH.

MARY (*to herself*): 'Captain Plume, I despise your listing-money; if I do serve, 'tis purely for love – of that wench I mean. For you must know,' etc –
    'So you only want an opportunity for accomplishing your designs upon her?'
    'Well, sir, I'm satisfied as to the point in debate; but now let me beg you to lay aside your recruiting airs, put on the man of honour, and tell me plainly what usage I must expect when I'm under your command.'

She tries that again, with a stronger and lower voice. RALPH *comes on, sees her. She sees him, but continues.*

'And something tells me, that if you do discharge me 'twill be the greatest punishment you can inflict; for were we this moment to go upon the greatest dangers in your profession, they would be less terrible to me than to stay behind you. – And now your hand, – this lists me – and now you are my captain.'

RALPH (*as* PLUME): 'Your friend'. (*Kisses her.*) ''Sdeath! There's something in this fellow that charms me.'

MARY: 'One favour I must beg – this affair will make some noise' –

RALPH: Silvia –

He kisses her again.

MARY: 'I must therefore take care to be impressed by the Act of Parliament –'

RALPH: 'What you please as to that. Will you lodge at my quarters in the meantime? You shall have part of my bed.' Silvia. Mary.

MARY: Am I doing it well? It's difficult to play a man. It's not the walk, it's the way you hold your head. A man doesn't bow his head so much and never at an angle. I must face you without lowering my head. Let's try it again.

RALPH: 'What you please as to that. – Will you lodge at my quarters in the meantime? You shall have part of my bed.' Mary!

She holds her head straight. Pause.

Will you?

Pause.

MARY: Yes.

They kiss.

RALPH: Don't lower your head. Silvia wouldn't.

She begins to undress, from the top.

I've never looked at the body of a woman before.

MARY: Your wife?

RALPH: It wasn't right to look at her. Let me see you.

MARY: Yes. Let me see you.

RALPH: Yes.

He begins to undress himself.

Scene Ten

The Question of Liz

RALPH, ROSS, PHILLIP, COLLINS, CAMPBELL.

COLLINS: She refused to defend herself at the trial. She didn't say a word. This was taken as an admission of guilt and she was condemned to be hanged. The evidence against her, however, is flimsy.

ROSS: She was seen with Kable next to the food stores. That is a fingering fact.

COLLINS: She was seen by a drunken soldier in the dark. He admitted he was drunk and that he saw her at a distance. He knew Kable was supposed to be repairing the door and she's known to be friends with Kable and Arscott. She won't speak, she won't say where she was. That is our difficulty.

ROSS: She won't speak because she's guilty.

PHILLIP: Silence has many causes, Robbie.

RALPH: She won't speak, Your Excellency, because of the convict code of honour. She doesn't want to beg for her life.

ROSS: Convict code of honour. This pluming play has muddled the muffy Lieutenant's mind.

COLLINS: My only fear, Your Excellency, is that she may have refused to speak because she no longer believes in the process of justice. If that is so, the courts here will become travesties. I do not want that.

PHILLIP: But if she won't speak, there is nothing more we can do. You cannot get at the truth through silence.

RALPH: She spoke to Harry Brewer.

PHILLIP: But Harry never regained consciousness before he died.

RALPH: James Freeman was there and told me what she said.

PHILLIP: Wasn't this used in the trial?

COLLINS: Freeman's evidence wasn't very clear and as Liz Morden wouldn't confirm what he said, it was dismissed.

ROSS: You can't take the word of a crooked crawling hangman.

PHILLIP: Why won't she speak?

ROSS: Because she's guilty. Hang her.

PHILLIP: Robbie, we may be about to hang the first woman in this colony, I do not want to hang the first innocent woman.

RALPH: We must get at the truth.

ROSS: Truth! We have 800 thieves, perjurers, forgers, murderers, liars, escapers, rapists, whores, coiners in this scrub-ridden, dust-driven, thunder-bolted, savage-run, cretinous colony. My marines who are trained to fight are turned into gouly gaolers, fed less than the prisoners –

PHILLIP: The rations, Major, are the same for all, prisoners and soldiers.

ROSS: They have a right to more so that makes them have less. Not a ship shifting into sight, the prisoners running away, stealing, drinking and the wee ductile Lieutenant talks about the truth.

PHILLIP: Truth is indeed a luxury, but its absence brings about the most abject poverty in a civilisation. That is the paradox.

ROSS: This is a profligate prison for us all, it's a hellish hole we soldiers have been hauled to because they blame us for losing the war in America. This is a hateful hary-scary, topsy-turvy outpost, this is not a civilisation. I hate this possumy place.

COLLINS: Perhaps we could return to the question of Liz Morden. (*Calls.*) Captain Campbell.

CAMPBELL *brings in* LIZ MORDEN.

COLLINS: Morden, if you don't speak, we will have to hang you; if you can defend yourself, His Excellency can overrule the court. We would not then risk a miscarriage of justice. But you must speak. Did you steal that food with the escaped prisoner Kable?

A long silence.

RALPH: She –

COLLINS: It is the accused who must answer.

PHILLIP: Liz Morden. You must speak the truth.

COLLINS: We will listen to you.

Pause.

RALPH: Morden. No one will despise you for telling the truth.

PHILLIP: That is not so, Lieutenant. Tell the truth and accept the contempt. That is the history of great men. Liz, you may be despised, but you will have shown courage.

RALPH: If that soldier has lied –

ROSS: There, there, he's accusing my soldiers of lying. It's that play, it makes fun of officers, it shows an officer lying and cheating. It shows a corrupt justice as well, Collins –

CAMPBELL: Good scene that, very funny, hah, scchhh.

COLLINS: Et tu, Campbell?

CAMPBELL: What? Meant only. Hahah. If he be so good at gunning he shall have enough – he may be of use against the French, for he shoots flying, hahaha. Good, and then there's this constable ha –

ROSS: Campbell!

PHILLIP: The play seems to be having miraculous effects already. Don't you want to be in it, Liz?

RALPH: Morden, you must speak.

COLLINS: For the good of the colony.

PHILLIP: And of the play.

A long silence.

LIZ: I didn't steal the food.

COLLINS: Were you there when Kable stole it?

LIZ: No. I was there before.

ROSS: And you knew he was going to steal it?

LIZ: Yes.

ROSS: Guilty. She didn't report it.

COLLINS: Failure to inform is not a hangable offence.

ROSS: Conspiracy.

COLLINS: We may need a retrial.

PHILLIP: Why wouldn't you say any of this before?

ROSS: Because she didn't have time to invent a lie.

COLLINS: Major, you are demeaning the process of law.

PHILLIP: Why, Liz?

LIZ: Because it wouldn't have mattered.

PHILLIP: Speaking the truth?

LIZ: Speaking.

ROSS: You are taking the word of a convict against the word of a soldier –

COLLINS: A soldier who was drunk and uncertain of what he saw.

ROSS: A soldier is a soldier and has a right to respect. You will have revolt on your hands, Governor.

PHILLIP: I'm sure I will, but let us see the play first. Liz, I hope you are good in your part.

RALPH: She will be, Your Excellency, I promise that.

LIZ: Your Excellency, I will endeavour to speak Mr Farquhar's lines with the elegance and clarity their own worth commands.

Scene Eleven

Backstage.

Night. THE ABORIGINE.

THE ABORIGINE: Look: oozing pustules on my skin, heat on my forehead. Perhaps we have been wrong all this time and this is not a dream at all.

The ACTORS *come on. They begin to change and make up.*

MARY: Are the savages coming to see the play as well?

KETCH: They come around the camp because they're dying: smallpox.

MARY: Oh.

SIDEWAY: I hope they won't upset the audience.

MARY: Everyone is here. All the officers too.

LIZ (*to* DUCKLING): Dabby could take your part.

DUCKLING: No. I will do it. I will remember the lines.

MARY: I've brought you an orange from Lieutenant Clark's island. They've thrown her out of Harry Brewer's tent.

WISEHAMMER: Why? He wouldn't have

wanted that.

DUCKLING: Major Ross said a whore was a whore and I was to go into the women's camp. They've taken all of Harry's things.

She bursts into tears.

MARY: I'll talk to the Lieutenant.

LIZ: Let's go over your lines. And if you forget them, touch my foot and I'll whisper them to you.

SIDEWAY (*who has been practising on his own*): We haven't rehearsed the bow. Garrick used to take his this way: you look up to the circle, to the sides, down, make sure everyone thinks you're looking at them. Get in a line.

They do so.

ARSCOTT: I'll be in the middle. I'm the tallest.

SIDEWAY: Dabby, you should be next to Mary.

DABBY: I won't take the bow.

SIDEWAY: It's not the biggest part, Dabby, but you'll be noticed.

DABBY: I don't want to be noticed.

SIDEWAY: Let's get this right. If we don't all do the same thing, it will look a mess.

They try. DABBY is suddenly transfixed.

DABBY: Hurray, hurray, hurray.

SIDEWAY: No, they will be shouting bravo, but we're not in a line yet.

DABBY: I wasn't looking at the bow, I saw the whole play, and we all knew our lines, and Mary, you looked so beautiful, and after that, I saw Devon and they were shouting bravo, bravo Dabby, hurray, you've escaped, you've sailed thousands and thousands of miles on the open sea and you've come back to your Devon, bravo Dabby, bravo.

MARY: When are you doing this, Dabby?

DABBY: Tonight.

MARY: You can't.

DABBY: I'll be in the play till the end, then in the confusion, when it's over, we can slip away. The tide is up, the night will be dark, everything's ready.

MARY: The Lieutenant will be blamed, I won't let you.

DABBY: If you say anything to the Lieutenant, I'll refuse to act in the play.

ARSCOTT: When I say my lines, I think of nothing else. Why can't you do the same?

DABBY: Because the play's only for one night. I want to grow old in Devon.

MARY: They'll never let us do another play, I'm telling the Lieutenant.

ALL: No, you're not.

DABBY: Please, I want to go back to Devon.

WISEHAMMER: I don't want to go back to England now. It's too small and they don't like Jews. Here, no one has more of a right than anyone else to call you a foreigner. I want to become the first famous writer.

MARY: You can't become a famous writer until you're dead.

WISEHAMMER: You can if you're the only one.

SIDEWAY: I'm going to start a theatre company. Who wants to be in it?

WISEHAMMER: I will write you a play about justice.

SIDEWAY: Only comedies, my boy, only comedies.

WISEHAMMER: What about a comedy about unrequited love?

LIZ: I'll be in your company, Mr Sideway.

KETCH: And so will I. I'll play all the parts that have dignity and gravity.

SIDEWAY: I'll hold auditions tomorrow.

DABBY: Tomorrow.

DUCKLING: Tomorrow.

MARY: Tomorrow.

LIZ: Tomorrow.

A long silence. (Un ange passe.)

MARY: Where are my shoes?

RALPH *comes in.*

RALPH: Arscott, remember to address the soldiers when you talk of recruiting. Look at them: you are speaking to them. And don't forget, all of you, to leave a space for people to laugh.

ARSCOTT: I'll kill anyone who laughs at me.

RALPH: They're not laughing at you, they're laughing at Farquhar's lines. You must expect them to laugh.

ARSCOTT: That's all right, but if I see Major Ross or any other officer laughing at me, I'll kill them.

MARY: No more violence. By the way, Arscott, when you carry me off the stage as Jack Wilful, could you be a little more gentle? I don't think he'd be so rough with a young gentleman.

RALPH: Where's Caesar?

KETCH: I saw him walking towards the beach earlier. I thought he was practising his lines.

ARSCOTT: Caesar!

He goes out.

WISEHAMMER (*to* LIZ): When I say 'Do you love fishing, madam?', do you say something then? –

RALPH (*goes over to* DUCKLING): I am so sorry, Duckling. Harry was my friend.

DUCKLING: I loved him. But now he'll never know that. I thought that if he knew he would become cruel.

RALPH: Are you certain you don't want Dabby to take your part?

DUCKLING: No! I will do it. I want to do it.

Pause.

He liked to hear me say my lines.

RALPH: He will be watching from somewhere. (*He goes to* MARY.) How beautiful you look.

MARY: I dreamt I had a necklace of pearls and three children.

RALPH: If we have a boy we will call him Harry.

MARY: And if we have a girl?

RALPH: She will be called Betsey Alicia.

ARSCOTT *comes in with* CAESAR *drunk and dishevelled.*

ARSCOTT: Lying on the beach, dead drunk.

CAESAR: I can't. All those people. My ancestors are angry, they do not want me to be laughed at by all those people.

RALPH: You wanted to be in this play and you will be in this play

KETCH: I'm nervous too, but I've overcome it. You have to be brave to be an actor.

CAESAR: My ancestors will kill me.

He swoons. ARSCOTT *hits him.*

ARSCOTT: You're going to ruin my first scene.

CAESAR: Please, Lieutenant, save me.

RALPH: Caesar, if I were back home, I wouldn't be in this play either. My ancestors wouldn't be very pleased to see me here with people not of –. But our ancestors are thousands of miles away.

CAESAR: I cannot be a disgrace to Madagascar.

ARSCOTT: You will be more of a disgrace if you don't come out with me on that stage NOW.

MARY: Think of us as your family

SIDEWAY (*to* RALPH): What do you think of this bow?

RALPH: Caesar, I am your Lieutenant and I command you to go on that stage. If you don't, you will be tried and hanged for treason.

KETCH: And I'll tie the rope in such a way you'll dangle there for hours full of piss and shit.

RALPH: What will your ancestors think of that, Caesar?

CAESAR *cries but pulls himself together.*

KETCH (*to* LIZ): I couldn't have hanged you.

LIZ: No?

RALPH: Dabby, have you got your chickens?

DABBY: My chickens? Yes. Here.

RALPH: Are you all right?

DABBY: Yes. (*Pause.*) I was dreaming.

RALPH: Of your future success?

DABBY: Yes. Of my future success.

RALPH: And so is everyone here, I hope. Now, Arscott.

ARSCOTT: Yes, Sir!

RALPH: Calm.

ARSCOTT: I have been used to danger, Sir.

SIDEWAY: Here.

LIZ: What's that?

SIDEWAY: Salt. For good luck.

RALPH: Where did you get that from?

SIDEWAY: I have been saving it from my rations. I have saved enough for each of us to have some.

They all take a little salt.

WISEHAMMER: Lieutenant?

RALPH: Yes, Wisehammer.

WISEHAMMER: There's – there's –

MARY: There's his prologue.

RALPH: The prologue. I forgot.

Pause.

Let me hear it again.

WISEHAMMER:
From distant climes o'er wide-spread seas
we come,
Though not with much éclat or beat of
drum,
True patriots all; for be it understood,
We left our country for our country's good;
No private views disgraced our generous
zeal,
What urg'd our travels was our country's
weal,
And none will doubt but that our
emigration
Has prov'd most useful to the British
nation.

Silence.

RALPH: When Major Ross hears that, he'll have an apoplectic fit.

MARY: I think it's very good.

DABBY: So do I. And true.

SIDEWAY: But not theatrical.

RALPH: It is very good, Wisehammer, it's very well written, but it's too-too political. It will be considered provocative.

WISEHAMMER: You don't want me to say it.

RALPH: Not tonight. We have many people against us.

WISEHAMMER: I could tone it down. I could omit 'We left our country for our country's good'.

DABBY: That's the best line.

RALPH: It would be wrong to cut it.

WISEHAMMER: I worked so hard on it.

LIZ: It rhymes.

SIDEWAY: We'll use it in the Sideway Theatre.

RALPH: You will get much praise as Brazen, Wisehammer.

WISEHAMMER: It isn't the same as writing.

RALPH: The theatre is like a small republic, it requires private sacrifices for the good of the whole. That is something you should agree with, Wisehammer.

Pause.

And now, my actors, I want to say what a pleasure it has been to work with you. You are on your own tonight and you must do your utmost to provide the large audience out there with a pleasurable, intelligible and memorable evening.

LIZ: We will do our best, Mr Clark.

MARY: I love this!

RALPH: Arscott.

ARSCOTT (*to* CAESAR): You walk three steps ahead of me. If you stumble once, you know what will happen to you later? Move?

RALPH: You're on.

ARSCOTT *is about to go on, then remembers:*

ARSCOTT: Halberd! Halberd!

He is handed his halberd and goes on, preceded by CAESAR *beating the drum.*